ELEGY

ANDREW ROBERTS is a prize-winning historian and one of Britain's most prominent journalists and broadcasters. His books include the critically acclaimed *Holy Fox: The Life of Lord Halifax* (1991); *Eminent Churchillians* (1994); *Salisbury: Victorian Titan* (1999), which won the Wolfson History Prize and the James Stern Silver Pen Award for Non-Fiction; *Hitler and Churchill: Secrets of Leadership* (2003); *Masters and Commanders: The Military Geniuses Who Led the West to Victory in World War II* (2008); *The Storm of War: A New History of the Second World War* (2010); and *Napoleon the Great* (2015), which coincided with a three-part BBC2 history series.

The Holy Fox: The Life of Lord Halifax

Eminent Churchillians

The Aachen Memorandum

Salisbury: Victorian Titan

Napoleon and Wellington

Hitler and Churchill:
Secrets of Leadership

What Might Have Been
   (*Editor*)

Waterloo: Napoleon's Last Gamble

The Correspondence Between Mr Disraeli
and Mrs Brydges Willyams
   (*Editor*)

A History of the English-Speaking Peoples
Since 1900

Masters and Commanders:
How Roosevelt, Churchill, Marshall
and Alanbrooke Won the War in the West

The Art of War: Great Commanders
of the Ancient and Medieval World
   (*Editor*)

The Art of War: Great Commanders
of the Modern World Since 1600
   (*Editor*)

The Storm of War: A New History
of the Second World War

Love, Tommy: Letters Home,
from the Great War to the Present Day
   (*Editor*)

Napoleon the Great

ROTATION STOCK

ANDREW ROBERTS
ELEGY

—

THE FIRST DAY ON THE SOMME

First published in the UK in 2015 by Head of Zeus Ltd

1 3 5 7 9 10 8 6 4 2

A catalogue record for this book is available
from the British Library.

ISBN (Hardback) 9781784080013
ISBN (eBook) 9781784080006

Designed by Ken Wilson | point918
Maps by Ki229

Printed and bound in Germany
by GGP Media GmbH, Pössneck

HEAD OF ZEUS LTD
Clerkenwell House
45–47 Clerkenwell Green
London ECIR OHT

www.headofzeus.com

To
JOHN LEE

CONTENTS

The Western Front from Nieuport to Verdun, 1916

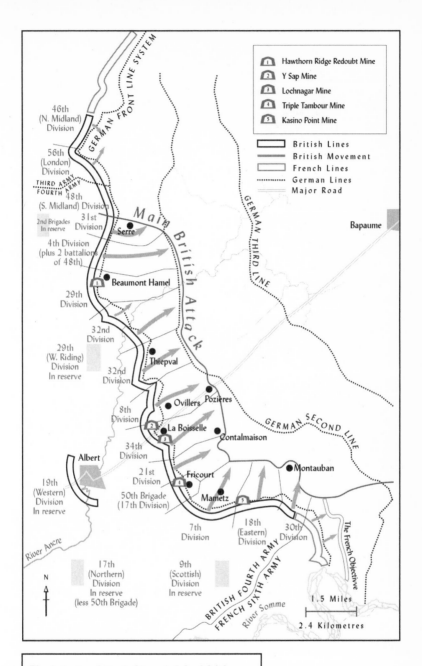

The Infantry Attack Plan, 1 July 1916

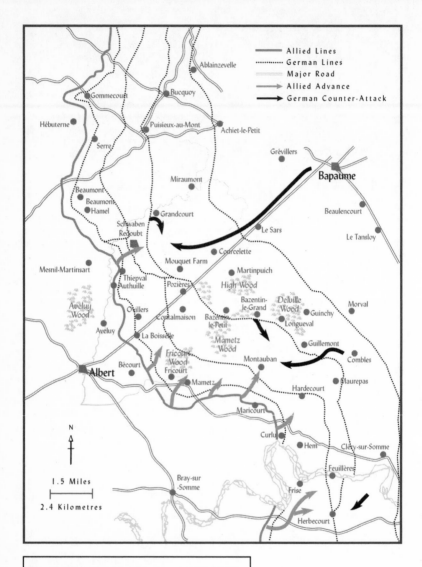

Allied Lines
German Lines
Major Road
Allied Advance
German Counter-Attack

Ablainzevelle
Gommecourt
Bucquoy
Hébuterne
Puisieux-au-Mont
Achiet-le-Petit
Serre
Grévillers
Bapaume
Miraumont
Beaumont
Beaulencourt
Beaumont
Hamel
Grandcourt
Le Tansloy
Schwaben
Redoubt
Le Sars
Mouquet Farm
Courcelette
Mesnil-Martinsart
Martinpuich
Thiepval
High Wood
Authuille
Pozières
Delville
Wood
Morval
Aveluy
Wood
Bazentin-
le-Grand
Guinchy
Ovillers
Contalmaison
Bazentin-
le-Petit
Longueval
Aveluy
Mametz
Wood
Guillemont
La Boisselle
Combles
Fricourt
Wood
Bécourt
Montauban
Fricourt
Maurepas
Albert
Mametz
Hardecourt
Maricourt
Curlu
Hem
Cléry-sur-Somme
Feuillères
N
Bray-sur-
Somme
Frise
1.5 Miles
Herbecourt
2.4 Kilometres

The Battlefield of the Somme, 1 July 1916

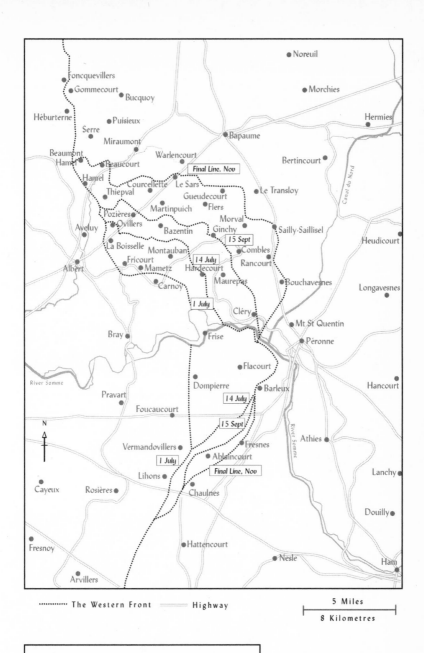

The Western Front, November 1916

INTRODUCTION

'We have made a covenant with Death
and with Hell we are in agreement.'

Isaiah 28:15

'HAS THE ENEMY'S FRONT LINE BEEN CAPTURED?' ASKED the commanding officer of the 1st Battalion of the Newfoundland Regiment, Lt.-Col. Arthur Hadow. The reply he received from his 88th Brigade headquarters was terse: 'The situation is not cleared up.' It was 8.45 a.m. on the morning of Saturday, 1 July 1916—a beautiful summer's morning with a clear blue sky—and Hadow had been given orders by his immediate superior, Brig. Douglas E. Cayley, to advance 'as soon as possible' to support the attack of the 87th Brigade on the German trenches situated in front of 'Y' Ravine at Beaumont Hamel north of the river Ancre in Picardy. He inquired whether 'as soon as possible' meant that he was expected to attack without the support of the 1st Battalion of the Essex Regiment on his right flank, and was told that it did.[1] The Newfoundlanders were going to have to attack alone.

The Newfoundlanders had been crouching in support trenches behind the front lines awaiting the signal to attack since long before dawn. They had made their way up from their billets behind the lines in the pretty French town of Louvencourt at 9 p.m. the previous evening, so that they would not need to spend more than one night in the crowded, wet, dangerous trenches mired in sticky, yellowish mud. As they had marched out of Louvencourt, one of the men attached to the Lewis machine gun unit, Pte. Charlie 'Ginger' Byrnes of the 2nd Battalion the Hampshire Regiment, noticed how 'Those people lining the village street, some of them were crying. Tears pouring

PICARDY LANDSCAPE
A watercolour by Louis Welden Hawkins (1849–1910) showing
the Somme countryside as it was before warfare destroyed it.

down their faces. Well, I thought to meself, that's cheerful, that
is. Right bloody cheerful, that's what.'[2]

The Newfoundlanders had written their wills before leaving
home. 'I am on the point of leaving for England to fight for a great
and just cause, for all that Englishmen the world over hold dear,'
wrote a second lieutenant from the island's capital, St John's,

in a word, for material existence. If am called upon to
lay down my life, I hope the glory of the cause will fully
comfort any who might mourn for me. I must record
my admiration for my dear wife's brave self-sacrifice,

4

devotion and unflinching courage. So far from trying to dissuade me from the duty which lay clear before me, she has by her noble self-control and sympathetic love given me the encouragement and help I always knew she would. Of my beloved parents I must add that none have ever enjoyed better, or ever will. May God bless and keep them well. Farewell.[3]

That young subaltern was killed in the Battle of Monchy-le-Preux in April 1917, but his sentiments were fully representative of those of his comrades who fell on the first day of the Somme Offensive.

The Newfoundlanders had marched up to their support trenches and dugouts at St John's Road (so named by the South Wales Borderers as a compliment) and Clonmel Avenue (named for the town in Tipperary) at 2 a.m. on 1 July, a full five-and-a-half hours before the general infantry assault timed for 7.30 a.m., 'Z Hour'. They were to form part of the second wave of the vast British assault, and were intended to attack at 10.40 a.m., passing through the first echelons of the 87th Brigade, comprising the 2nd South Wales Borderers and 1st Border Regiment, and then regrouping on Station Road far behind enemy lines, before going on to capture Puisieux Trench a full 2 miles (3.2 km) away.[4] That was the original plan, at least; in fact no-one in either brigade was even so much as to glimpse Station Road that day.

'For officers there was no rest', recalled the Newfoundlanders' adjutant, Capt. Arthur Raley MC,

> but the men, very tired after five hours marching, were soon asleep except of course for sentries, etc. Lewis gunners overhauled their guns and each man was roused

5

in turn to have his equipment inspected. Another tedious
duty was the issuing of further battle stores to those
previously detailed to carry them. These stores consisted
chiefly of trench bridges and ladders, to be carried by two
men each, and Bangalore torpedoes... With inspections
and issues of stores having been completed, there was
only the wait for Zero Hour... Most of the men dozed,
the officers strolled about their various commands chat-
ting to groups in each firebay and giving final little bits of
advice. Cigarette smoking was allowed and altogether it
was very much like the final few minutes before a big football match. The British artillery was keeping up a continuous roar; so much firing was going on that the sharp
crack of the field guns was almost reduced to nothing by
the ceaseless rush of the shells overhead. Slowly the sky
in the East grew lighter and as day broke a last meal was
taken by all ranks... At 6 a.m. everybody was alert and the
final wait had commenced.[5]

At 6.30 a.m. the men heard what Capt. Raley described as 'the
hurricane bombardment' of the German front-line trenches as
the now seven-day-long barrage against the enemy's positions
built to a crescendo. 'The noise was now kept at a steady pitch;
there was no break in the sound at all; in fact it seemed as if the
sound was felt rather than heard, the air suddenly seeming to
increase in weight.'[6] It had been the heaviest bombardment in
the history of warfare.

Officers synchronized their watches at 7.15 a.m. and then at
7.20 a.m. troops on both sides of no man's land heard the tremendous explosion of an enormous mine on Hawthorn Ridge
only a thousand yards (914 m) away from the Newfoundlanders'
trenches. Ten minutes later the sound of other units' officers

blowing their whistles signalled the first attack in the 'Big Push' that everyone—Germans, Britons, Newfoundlanders alike— had been expecting for months.

The ear-splitting sound of German artillery shells hitting the Newfoundlanders' own positions, however, soon made it clear that the enemy's guns had not been silenced, as the men had been assured that they would. Furthermore, trench raids over the previous few days had discovered that the British artillery bombardment had not cut through the dense rolls of barbed wire in no man's land as deeply as the gunners had hoped. Worst of all, the huge number of wounded men hobbling and crawl- ing back from the 87th Brigade's initial attack soon told its own worrying story, for within a few minutes it had suffered over two thousand casualties without even reaching the wire. Yet the Newfoundlanders were not downhearted; they had waited for over two years to get to grips with the enemy, and this would be their chance.

Because the wounded of 87th Brigade were entirely blocking the communication trenches that the Newfoundlanders needed to use in order to reach the front line, the decision was taken that they would have to attack from the support trenches in which they were now congregated, a full 250 yards (228 m) to the rear of the frontline assembly trenches. Collecting his com- pany commanders together for a quick conference at 8.45 a.m., Hadow explained that there was now no time to come up with any new tactics for the changed situation, so the assault would have to use the same formation that had been practised for three weeks behind the lines at Louvencourt, whereby A and B Com- panies moved forward in lines abreast, followed by C and D

Companies. The attack would have to cover the extra distance to the Newfoundlanders' own front line in the open. Orders to subalterns and non-commissioned officers were relayed, and at 9.15 a.m. Brigade Headquarters (HQ) was told: 'The Newfoundlanders are moving.'[7]

Hadow climbed out of the trench first, carrying, as he always did, his thick ash walking stick. When he had advanced 20 yards (18 m) he gave the signal and, in the words of one observer, 'immediately the parapet swarmed with men. From each corner of every traverse [trench] men came pouring. With remarkable precision they took up their correct position in their sections.'[8] For the first minute or so, it was a textbook operation.

MUD
Although mud was not a factor on the first day of the Somme Offensive, it was an almost ubiquitous feature in Western Front trench warfare.

Morale was high: when the news had got round that a rich society beauty from St John's had promised to marry the first member of the regiment to win a Victoria Cross (VC), the single men had made up a battle cry with which they now went over the top: 'Buxom Bessie or a wooden leg!' The regimental historian recorded how, 'All appeared to be in excellent spirits and confident in their ability to do the task assigned them.'[9] Only a few days earlier, on 26 June, the commander of 29th Division, Maj.-Gen. Henry de Beauvoir de Lisle, had addressed the Newfoundland Regiment on parade and told them that the British 4th Army would fire 45,000 tons (40,823 tonnes) of ammunition at the German trenches, enough shells, he said, to fill 46 miles (74 km) of railway trucks. He added that the British Expeditionary Force (BEF) and French army's 263 battalions on the Somme faced only thirty-two German battalions, which it would take the enemy a full week to reinforce. Lt. Owen Steele summarized the general's speech with the words, 'So we need fear nothing.' The fact that the Germans actually had thirty-three regiments, each consisting of the equivalent of three battalions, was either not known by de Lisle or not mentioned by him.[10]

At divisional HQ after 7.30 a.m. on 1 July, de Lisle had somehow come to the early conclusion that his attacks were going far better than they were. Observers had exaggerated the strength of the groups from 87th Brigade that were moving forward unchecked, and crucially there were also reports of white flares being fired into the air, the signal that frontline trenches had been captured. He therefore ordered his reserve 88th Brigade under Brig.-Gen. Cayley to send two battalions behind the 87th along the Beaumont Hamel–Auchonvillers road. They were to attack without artillery support, with only a barrage from the 88th Machine Gun Company to suppress enemy fire.[11] It later transpired that the white flares had in fact been fired by the Germans in the front-line trenches to signal to their own artillery that shells were falling short.[12]

Cayley's orders to Hadow had been to advance from St John's Road and Clonmel Avenue and pass through the narrow gaps in the four belts of British barbed wire that covered a slight hill running down towards the German trenches and then penetrate the Germans' barbed wire in the middle of no man's land—and all in broad daylight. 'A more deadly piece of ground to cross it is hard to imagine,' recalled Capt. Raley. 'From the very start it was obvious that the enemy were not only extremely well prepared for an attack but were actually expecting it... Before the Newfoundland officer had finished synchronizing his watch, wounded men of the South Wales Borderers were flopping back over the parapet. In spite of our tremendous gunfire the enemy machine gunners and riflemen were firing as only well-trained men could.' As well as being heavily wired, the German defences in front of Beaumont Hamel were deeply dug in, with Y Ravine in particular boasting many deep shelters. To the east, the ridge gave the Germans perfect observation of every movement in and from the British trenches.[13] From the German trenches at Y Ravine at Beaumont Hamel today, it is easy to spot with the naked eye individuals standing where the Newfoundlanders' trenches were sited.

'It was daylight by then,' recalled 'Ginger' Byrnes of the moments just prior to going over the top,

GERMAN DUGOUT

*The Germans' dugouts on the Somme were far deeper and more
sophisticated than the British and French suspected.*

lovely morning it was. I heard the rattle of machine gun
fire: you could always hear that above everything else.
After a while the [87th Brigade's] wounded started…
streaming down in fours and fives, one fellow helping
another along; there didn't seem to be any end to them.
You got to thinking there couldn't be many left out there.
Of course you can't see anything from the bottom of a
trench. So we moved out of the way for the wounded… I
put the ammo box over my shoulder, thinking, I dunno!
If we're going, I wish we'd go and get it over with. But
still we stayed there. The officer came back, then went
away. He did this about four times at about twenty minute
intervals. He kept on looking at his watch. The last time
he appeared he said 'Come on lads. Time we went.' They
had a scaling ladder in this bay: that was a wooden ladder
with about four rungs. The officer went first, then the
other two chaps, then me. Of course I had those ruddy
ammo boxes and my rifle, so I didn't go over the top with
dash you might say—more of a humping and scrambling
really. No yelling 'Charge' or anything like that. I kept
my eye on the officer ahead. He turned to wave us fellers
on and then down he went—just as though he was bloody
pole-axed. I just kept moving… there were blokes lying
everywhere.[14]

The men set off at 9.15 a.m. in the direction which today can be
traced from the splendid statue of a defiant caribou at the Beaumont Hamel Memorial Park towards what is now the Y Ravine
cemetery. Within moments of clambering out of their trenches
and dressing their lines, they were submitted to a devastating machine gun barrage that scythed men down long before
they could even reach their own front line. German Maxim
machine guns were capable of firing 500 bullets a minute, and

the shape of the German trench line they were attacking in Y Ravine meant that the Newfoundlanders were caught in a concave front, with the enemy able to deliver enfilading crossfire as well as a direct frontal fusillade. The tiered German defences at Beaumont Hamel allowed their machine guns to cover the whole British front from no fewer than three separate supporting lines of trenches.[15] Y Ravine ran east–west, but vitally it had a pronounced salient around its head, meaning that if it was not destroyed or captured early on, the machine guns there would also be able to pour enfilading fire on men attacking either side of it. The 2nd South Wales Borderers were destroyed in a matter of a few minutes after Z Hour, and in that time the gaps in the wire were revealed to the German machine gunners.[16]

GERMAN MACHINE GUNNERS
An enemy gun position on 15 July 1916: the amount of overhead cover suggests it is part of the German second main line position.

Just as disastrously, the machine guns from all around the sector could now concentrate entirely on the Newfoundlanders, since the 1st Essex Regiment would not be ready to attack for another forty minutes due to the total congestion of its trenches by the wounded from 87th Brigade. One artillery observer reported that the Newfoundlanders were dropping dead and wounded at every yard, yet the battalion pressed on without faltering. To make matters worse, because the commander of VIII Corps, to which 88th Brigade belonged, Lt.-Gen. Sir Aylmer Hunter-Weston, had, along with so many others in the High Command, convinced himself that the preliminary bombardment would destroy the German positions, the men had been ordered to advance at walking pace to conserve energy, and were loaded down with an average of 66 lbs (30 kg) of equipment each. 'The only visible sign that the men knew they were under this terrific fire', wrote Raley, 'was that they instinctively tucked their chins into an advanced shoulder as they had done so often when fighting their way home in a blizzard in some little outpost in far off Newfoundland.'[17]

Despite attacking without artillery support across half a mile (0.8 km) of downward-sloping open ground in full view and range of the German machine guns and other ordnance, Capt. Jim Ledingham's A Company and Joe Nunns' B Company got through the second and third belts of British barbed wire, albeit with heavy losses. A hundred yards (91.4 m) behind them Capt. Rex Rowsell's C Company came on, carrying picks and shovels as well as rifles and bayonets, and next to them D Company. It was only once A and B Companies got through the British wire that they could even see the German trenches hundreds of yards ahead of them, scars and slight ramparts in the earth beyond the German wire. Captain Nunns was shot in the leg when he had gone just beyond the British wire and ordered a subaltern, Lt. Hubert Herder, to take command of the company. Picking up his platoon sergeant's rifle and bayonet—the Newfoundland officers had gone into action carrying revolvers—Herder shouted 'Come on, boys!' before being mortally wounded himself.[18]*

By then German artillery—largely untouched by counter-battery fire from the Royal Artillery—was pouring shrapnel across the 750 yards (686 m) of front that the Newfoundlanders were attacking, and the corpses of young soldiers were piling up around a clump of trees and stumps bereft of leaves, including the petrified skeleton of one that is still there today, known as the 'Danger Tree'.

Small parties that did manage to make it there, and orientate themselves towards a gap in the German wire, drew the machine-gunners' special attention, not least because they were silhouetted on the horizon and hard to miss. Near that tree fell Frank Lind, who two days earlier had written a letter to the *Daily News* back home saying, 'Tell everyone that they may feel proud of the Newfoundland Regiment.'

'Men were falling faster now,' recalled Raley, 'the machine gun fire was appallingly heavy but the steadiness of the men was quite unshaken. On they went with never so much as a waver anywhere. Each man as he fell, if life was still in him, endeavoured

---

* He is among forty-five Newfoundlanders buried in Y Ravine cemetery, one of three Commonwealth War Graves in the Beaumont Hamel Memorial Park.

to roll out of the way of his comrades, there to lie until those wonderful Newfoundland stretcher-bearers found them.'

'It seemed impossible that men could live to get through those gaps,' another observer recalled,

> yet here and there a man could be seen to dash forward as if bursting through a hedge. Here and there could be seen an officer, looking for men to lead. They were through the last belt now, but oh! how few… In one case, towards the left of the line, a section advanced on the last belt almost intact—or possibly others had joined it. In the rear of this last section walked two men carrying a ten-foot [3 m] trench bridge. As the section approached the gap, the leading man of the two was hit and, as he fell, brought down the bridge and his partner. Without the least sign of flurry, the second man got up, hoisted the bridge onto his head and slowly picked his way through the now-crowded gap. Whether the German machine gunners withheld their fire in admiration is not known but this hero stolidly advanced until he could advance no further.[19]

Virtually no men reached the German barbed wire, let alone their trenches, and those who did were cut down before they reached the parapet.[20]

The contemporaneous regimental war diary states:

> The distance to our objective varied from 650 to 900 yards [595 to 823 m]. The enemy's fire was effective from the outset but the heaviest casualties occurred on passing through the gaps in our front wire where the men were mowed down in heaps. Many more gaps in the wire were required than had been cut. In spite of the losses the survivors steadily advanced close to the enemy's wire by

which time very few remained. A few men are believed
to have actually succeeded in throwing bombs into the
enemy's trench.'[21]

This cannot be verified, however. A rumour credits a Pte.
Thomas Carroll with reaching the German trenches.[22] 'No
words of mine can give a fair account of the advance', wrote their
proud but heartbroken adjutant, who won a Croix de Guerre to
add to his Military Cross. 'It was just a steady walk forward of
several hundred Newfoundlanders, each one knowing that he
was going to be hit but determined to carry out his orders until
he could advance no further.'

The scene in the Beaumont Hamel trenches during and
after the attack was truly dreadful. 'The trenches were literally
packed with the wounded and dead of all regiments', recalled
an eyewitness. 'The heat was unbearable and added to this was
the incessant bursting of heavy shells on parapet, traverse and
in the trench. Wounded men who had managed to crawl a little
rolled down into the trench, falling with a sickening thud on the
bottom or some wounded comrade and they lay there under a
sweltering sun, groaning and waiting for a stretcher-bearer.'[23]

Before the attack, metal triangles of 18-inch (46 cm) sides
made from biscuit tins had been stitched onto the men's backs
in order to help the British forward observation officers plot the
advance of the infantry, but these glinted in the sunlight when
the men tried to get back to British lines from no man's land,
attracting the German machine gunners' attention.

The universal question asked by the men as they got back to the
trenches, wounded or not, was 'Is the Colonel satisfied? Is the

BEAUMONT HAMEL

The terrain which the Newfoundlanders, 1st Essex and others had to try to cross in the teeth of German machine gun fire.

Colonel pleased?'[24] It was asked without a trace of irony. Hadow was indeed pleased with their heroism, but within twenty minutes it was clear that the battalion had been effectively destroyed with absolutely nothing to show for it, and at 9.45 a.m., only half an hour after the attack began, he had to report to Brig.-Gen. Cayley at brigade headquarters, a hundred yards (91.4 m) behind the British firing line, that the attack had completely failed. 'Shortly afterwards,' the regimental war diary recorded, '[the] enemy opened an intense bombardment of our trenches with heavy artillery which was kept up for some time.'[25]

The Newfoundlanders' losses were horrific—89 per cent of the men who went over the top had been either killed or wounded, including all of their twenty-six officers.* Nonetheless, Cayley ordered Hadow to gather together any unwounded

---

* The battalion lost three more officers than should have gone into action because they volunteered to take part despite not being required to by their duties.

Newfoundlanders that he could find, and attack the German positions once again.[26] Hadow dutifully returned to the trenches looking for enough men to carry out what amounted to a suicide attack, but the order was fortunately countermanded in time by a senior staff officer from VIII Corps HQ.

For Hadow and his decimated regiment, at least, the bloodiest day in the history of the British army was almost over. Cayley nevertheless still ordered the 1st Essex to go over the top at 9.55 a.m.; in the words of the war diarist, 'i.e. after our attack had failed'.[27] They also suffered terribly, but it was not until Maj.-Gen. de Lisle heard at 10.05 a.m. of the total failure of his two leading brigades that he called off further attacks, at least until he ordered the 4th Worcesters to try to capture the Y Ravine salient at 12.30 p.m., although the impossibility of carrying out that order was also recognized in time. Instead, the order was given to prepare for a German counter-attack that never transpired.

Attached to the Newfoundlanders' war diary is a statement from Capt. G.E. Malcolm, who commanded D Company of the 1st Battalion King's Own Scottish Borderers, which formed part of the first attack of the 87th Brigade, who wrote to his adjutant: 'I should like to congratulate the Newfoundland Regiment on their extreme steadiness under trying conditions'[28]—a form of British understatement that has rarely been exceeded.

'During the night and evening,' recorded the war diary, 'unwounded survivors managed to crawl back to our own lines and by next morning some 68 had answered their names, in addition to stretcher-bearers and HQ runners.'[29] The men left out in no man's land after the collapse of the attack suffered badly from thirst during that warm summer's day. They could not move back for fear of snipers and machine guns. Pte. Byrnes, whose entire machine gun team had been killed, found himself a shell-hole: 'a nice new shell-hole—it wasn't big, but I couldn't see a better one handy. I was only young—nineteen. There was no-one to give any orders... I slung the ammunition boxes down and dived into it... And there I stayed all day'[30] He recorded how out in no man's land, 'One man lost his head and stood up and tried to run back. He'd got a terrible wound in his leg and what with the heat and everything I expect he'd gone barmy. He'd got one leg dragging and he tried to get back. He didn't get far. He got peppered. He was dead. You could see the sun glinting on the tin triangles some of them had [on] their backs... I lay there and watched it all... It was a long, long day.'[31]

That night, with the Germans putting up flares so that their machine gunners could fire at anything that moved, Byrne crawled back 'not on hands and knees, but toes and elbows, hugging the ground. It was slow work.' He abandoned everything but his gas mask as he crawled from shell-hole to shell-hole, back through the gaps in the wire and eventually into the Newfoundlanders' trench in one piece. The next day an informal truce allowed many of the wounded who had survived the night to be evacuated from no man's land. Over the next week, the Newfoundlanders buried their dead, sometimes in abandoned trenches.[32]

Their parents were later able to leave messages on their gravestones: George and Jessie Reid of St John's, parents of Sgt. Charles Reid, chose 'He died that others might live.' In the Y Ravine cemetery lies Pte. C.F.Taylor, who was twenty-three, whose parents chose this text: 'His last words when leaving home were I have only once to die.' Nearby in that cemetery lies LCpl. C. Smalley, of the South Wales Borderers, aged nineteen. His widowed mother, Elizabeth Smalley of Warrington, wrote: 'Oh for a touch of a vanished hand and a sound of a voice that is stilled.'

'More success would probably have attended our efforts had we surprised the enemy by an attack at dawn', wrote Maj.-Gen. de Lisle ten days later, 'and had we concentrated our artillery fire on the first objective, leaving the second objective to be dealt with in a subsequent operation.'[33] A total of 8,408 infantrymen, including 226 officers, had gone over the top from the three brigades of his 29th Division on 1 July. Of these, 185 officers (or 82 per cent) and 4,926 other ranks (60 per cent) were casualties by the end of the day.[34] For the Newfoundlanders in particular, the statistics were even worse: of the 801 men of the Newfoundland Regiment who went over the top, 266 were killed and 446 wounded.[35] Hardly a family on the island was untouched by the massacre at Beaumont Hamel. Some lost two, three or even four members that day.* The Newfoundland casualties were only exceeded proportionately by one other battalion in the British army, the 10th West Yorkshires of 17th Division.[36]

As well as being the only non-Regular unit in the 29th Division, the 1st Battalion Newfoundland Regiment was the only non-British unit of the 3rd and 4th Armies to take part in the offensive on 1 July. It was not part of the Canadian army because Newfoundland was Britain's oldest colony—settled by John Cabot in 1497 and annexed to the crown in 1583—and did not join Canada until 1949. On the day that Britain declared war on Germany on 4 August 1914, the governor of Newfoundland, Walter Davidson, sent the British government a telegram saying that the colony would immediately supply 500 men to the war effort, even though at the time the 42,000 sq. mile (108,780 sq. km), 242,000-person island had no standing army, militia, nor even a government office.[37] Instead there were local voluntary Christian organizations such as the Church Lads' Brigade, the Catholic Cadet Corps and the Methodist Guards, which along with other groups formed the Newfoundland Patriotic Association, which raised the number of men promised by their governor. Even though Newfoundland itself was in no danger from Germany or the other Central Powers, her young men volunteered in droves to defend what was then still widely thought of as 'the Mother Country'.

The regiment had trained on the old cricket grounds on the

---

* Charles Robert Ayre, who owned the department store chain Ayre & Sons in St John's, lost four of his five grandsons.

north side of the Quidi Vidi Pond in the military encampment at Pleasantville, Newfoundland. The initial contingent of 537 men of the 1st Newfoundland Contingent wore Australian slouch hats, Canadian army overcoats and the distinctive blue puttees that were worn by the Church Lads' Brigade.* In October 1914 they crossed the Atlantic in the converted sealing ship *Florizel*, part of a Canadian convoy 9 miles (14.5 km) long and three abreast, landing at Devonport, the naval base near Plymouth. Meanwhile Davidson told his superiors in London that the men were 'very hardy and accustomed to hard work and little food'.[38] They trained for a year on Salisbury Plain because the clay plains were thought to be similar to what they would find in Flanders. Transferred to Scotland for further training, they were joined by another thousand reinforcements from home. In September 1915 the regiment arrived at Suvla Bay in Gallipoli, just as the campaign there was winding down. They were soon evacuated, and so had lost only thirty-eight men killed by early January 1916. They arrived on the Somme via Cairo that April.

After the Battle of the Somme, Lt.-Col. Hadow, who had taken over as commanding officer in December 1915 and had the reputation of being a strict disciplinarian, rebuilt the regiment with a large draft of new men. With his second-in-command, Maj. James Forbes-Robinson, who was to end the war with a VC, DSO and Bar and MC, he subjected the regiment to long training parades, which on occasion could last from 5.30 a.m. to 7.30 p.m. Hadow restored them to full fighting efficiency, and the battalion went on to follow up the breakthrough at the

---

* Although their blue puttees were replaced with khaki ones, the nickname 'Blue Puttees' stuck.

Battle of Arras in April 1917, losing 460 men in a few hours at Monchy-le-Preux, then smashing through the German army's great series of defensive fortifications known as the Hindenburg Line after the Battle of Cambrai that November. On 1 December 1917 they lost more than 400 men in the German counter-attack, and they fought at Passchendaele twice and at the Battle of Lys in 1918. Of the 4,212 Newfoundlanders who fought on the Western Front in the First World War, no fewer than 1,300 were killed.[39] After the war, Basil Gotto sculpted five magnificent bronze caribou memorials to the Newfoundland dead, which can be found at their bloodiest battlefields.

Writing to the prime minister of Newfoundland about the performance of the regiment on the first day of the Somme Offensive, Maj.-Gen. de Lisle said: 'It was a magnificent display of trained and disciplined valour, and its assault only failed of success because dead men can advance no further.'[40] It was true, but Hadow's vital question—'Has the enemy's front line been captured?'—was all too often answered in the negative that day. The brigade's battle plan had been based on the assumption that Y Ravine would be virtually clear of living Germans by the end of the week-long bombardment. The Newfoundlanders' experience on 1 July 1916 therefore echoed many of those battalions in the north and centre of the battlefield which, ordered to advance at no more than walking pace and weighed down by almost half their body weight in equipment, were methodically massacred by an annihilating machine gun, rifle and artillery fire that should have been silenced beforehand. For all too many men who served along the 18-mile-wide (29 km) battlefield, that is the simple, tragic story of the first day of the Somme.

ONE

STRATEGY

'Trenches and barbed wire fastened their
paralyzing grip on the field… war sank into the lowest
depths of beastliness and degeneration. The wonder of war,
the glory of war, the art of war all hung on its
shifting scenery. For years the armies had to eat, drink,
sleep among their own putrefactions.'[1]

GEN. SIR IAN HAMILTON

*

'We had "Gott Mit Uns" on our belt buckles,
but we still lost the war.'[2]

GFT HUGO VAN EGEREN,
55th Reserve Regiment

THE ORDERS GIVEN TO GEN. SIR DOUGLAS HAIG WERE as crisp as the seams on his staff officers' trousers. 'I was to keep friendly with the French,' he noted in his diary after a meeting with Lord Kitchener at the War Office in Whitehall on Friday, 3 December 1915. 'General Joffre should be looked upon as the C-in-C... In France we must do all we can to meet [Joffre's] wishes whatever may be our personal feelings about the French Army and its Commanders.' Kitchener was not a man to cross, and as Secretary of State for War he had the final say over whether Haig would be given the job of commander-in-chief of the BEF, the post Haig had been angling for ever since the current occupier, Sir John French, had badly mishandled the Battle of Loos that October. Kitchener was older than Haig, a military hero since Victorian days, an earl, the man on ten thousand recruitment posters and the proud possessor of an even more luxuriant moustache than Haig's own.

At the meeting Kitchener had confirmed that he 'had taken the matter in hand' and would be pressing the prime minister, Herbert Asquith, to give Sir John French's job to Haig over the next few days, so, as Haig recorded, 'I must not trouble my head over it. As soon as I was in the saddle he would see me again.' Such was Kitchener's confidence and invulnerable position in public esteem that he told Haig he 'must not be afraid to criticize any of his actions which I found unsatisfactory: he had only one thought, viz. to do his best to end the war.'[3] Beyond replacing his superior, that was Haig's main thought too, but when he left the War Office that day, he was under no illusions but that he would be implementing General Joseph Joffre's overall strategy once he got the job he craved.

Sir Douglas (later Field Marshal Earl) Haig is easily the most controversial commander-in-chief in British history. It could hardly be otherwise with the man whose battle plans were responsible both for the slaughter of the Somme in 1916 and Passchendaele a year later but also for the stunning series of victories on the Western Front that sealed Germany's fate in the last hundred days of the war in 1918. His reputation has veered between mass national veneration—his funeral in February 1928 was the largest since the Duke of Wellington's—and denigration of him as a callous, ignorant war criminal in Alan Clark's book *The Donkeys*, written in 1961 and immensely influential in popular culture, as the TV comedy series *Blackadder Goes Forth* showed to such absurdly poignant effect.[4]

Douglas Haig was fifty-five years old when he was appointed commander-in-chief of the BEF in December 1915. He came from a Scottish whisky distilling family, and had gone to Clifton College, Bristol, then Brasenose College, Oxford, and on to the British Army's officer training establishment at Sandhurst. A cavalryman, he had done well in the 1898 Sudan campaign and, unlike many British officers, also distinguished himself in the Boer War. Far from being the hidebound reactionary idiot of popular misconception, he was an Army reformer who had collaborated with the visionary Secretary of State for War, Richard Haldane, between 1905 and 1912. These reforms created the

ROYAL AIRCRAFT FACTORY FE2B
*A British two-seater biplane fighter; it came into service in late 1915
and saw action during the Somme Offensive.*

Territorial Army and the British Expeditionary Force, among
other innovations, and as director of military training Haig
wrote *Field Service Regulations*, the first-ever tactical manual for
the British army. He taught himself French, and some historians believe that he was more fluent in that language than in
English; he has been described as 'a reserved, tongue-tied Low-
land Scot... positively incoherent once he strayed off a written
paper'.[5] He was highly enthusiastic about and supportive of new
inventions that he hoped might provide his longed for breakthrough on the Western Front, such as mortar shells for smoke-
screens, wireless sets, poison gas, aeroplanes, and of course
tanks, which he championed from the start, unlike some other
cavalry officers.* The accusation that he thought machine guns

---

* On occasion he was over-enthusiastic and expected too much of first-
generation technology; he once fell for a charlatan who claimed to have invented
a death-ray.

were overrated, or ever said that two per battalion were enough, has also been comprehensively discredited.[6] He might not have been a particularly endearing person but generals do not need to be; much more importantly, he had a burning desire to win the most vicious conflict in human history, which had become an immovable war of position by the autumn of 1914.

When war broke out in 1914, Haig commanded I Corps, which he took to France, and at the end of that year he was promoted to command the newly formed 1st Army. He led a brilliant defence of Ypres in late 1914, where he repulsed the German attempt to reach the Channel coast. In late October 1915, after French's fiasco at the Battle of Loos, Haig told King George V that French was 'a source of great weakness to the army, and no-one had any faith in him anymore.'[7] It was one of those unusual cases when he who wielded the dagger wore the crown, and Haig replaced French on 19 December 1915.

Haig was never short of enemies, especially amongst Liberal politicians in the British government. In his book *Great Contemporaries*, Winston Churchill, who was First Lord of the Admiralty when the war broke out, compares Haig to

> a great surgeon before the days of anaesthetics, versed in every detail of such science as was known to him: sure of himself, steady of poise, knife in hand, intent upon the operation; entirely removed in his professional capacity from the agony of the patient, the anguish of relations, or the doctrines of rival schools, the devices of quacks, or the first-fruits of new learning... If the patient died, he would not reprove himself. It must be understood that I speak only of his professional actions. Once out of the theatre, his heart was as warm as any man's.[8]

Churchill undermined any praise of Haig with waspish qualifications such as: 'If Haig's mind was conventional, his character also displayed the qualities of the average, decent man, concentrated and magnified... He was rarely capable of rising to great heights; he was always incapable of falling below his standards.'[9]* There had long been bad blood between the two men, partly because Haig refused Churchill command of a brigade which Sir John French had promised him, and gave him a mere battalion instead.

Haig was also criticized by later commentators, many of them serious figures such as the military historians Sir Basil Liddell Hart and Professor Sir Michael Howard. 'The German General Staff used to divide army officers into four categories,' the latter has written, 'the clever and lazy, the clever and hard-working, the stupid and lazy and the stupid and hard-working. The clever and lazy made the best generals, the clever and hard-working the best staff-officers, the stupid and lazy could be fitted in as regimental officers; but the stupid and hard-working were a positive menace and had to be got rid of as quickly as possible. Douglas Haig belonged to the fourth group.'[10]

Haig was certainly hard-working, and almost obsessive about detail: in the 3rd Battle of Ypres he concerned himself with the cost of the stones that the French were supplying for road repairs. Yet he wasn't a château-general either, preferring to live in spartan conditions and refusing to emulate Asquith's recourse to brandy when the prime minister visited his headquarters. A

---

* Writing in his diary in August 1916—without giving any evidence—Haig stated that 'Winston's head is gone from taking drugs'.[11]

devout Christian, Haig was interested in fundamentalist religion and spiritualism; as a young officer, he had been put in touch with Napoleon by a spiritualist, and on the Western Front a Presbyterian chaplain persuaded him that he was carrying out God's will.[12]

Often depicted as heartless butcher, Haig was in fact anything but. Haig's diaries are littered with references to him visiting hospitals of every description—once nine in one day, plus three veterinary hospitals, yet it took a tough commander to show the necessarily stern exterior to keep up morale during terrible losses. He can be criticized for over-optimism before

GENERAL SIR DOUGLAS HAIG
*Commander of the British Expeditionary Force, Haig was
a highly educated soldier and a moderniser.*

and during the Somme Offensive, but excessive confidence was rife amongst his High Command, especially in the opening stages, and this can be partly blamed on the Intelligence team he gathered around himself, as we shall see.

By the winter of 1914/15, after it had been made clear at the Battle of the Marne the preceding summer that the Germans were not going to break through and capture Paris as their Schlieffen Plan had envisaged, a continuous line of trenches stretched over 400 miles (644 km) from the Swiss border to the English Channel, likened by the historian John Keegan to a long scar across the face of north-western Europe. The question therefore facing the British and French High Commands was straightforward: how to win the war against the most powerful military-industrial power in Europe, one that already controlled almost all of Belgium and eleven *départments* of northern France? Sitting still was not an option, and the Gallipoli adventure to try to turn the line of the Central Powers in Turkey had turned into an unqualified disaster by December 1915. The French were forced to counter-attack on the Western Front because so much of their national territory was occupied; as one British historian has put it, 'The British equivalent would have been the German army entrenched at Canterbury'.[13]

If there was a way of fighting the First World War that did not involve trying to smash frontally through formidable enemy defences, neither side discovered one. This was Haig's dilemma. As the war diarist of X Corps was to put it succinctly after the Battle of the Somme: 'The vast number of troops employed in this war have enabled both sides to prepare and occupy lines from Switzerland to the sea, leaving no flank to be turned and no room for envelopment and manoeuvre; the offensive must take the form of a frontal attack.'[14] The Dardanelles defeat had failed to knock the Ottoman empire out of the war, and the Russians had failed to make significant headway in Eastern Europe, so the struggle was clearly going to be a long, hard slog focused on the north-west of the continent and to a lesser extent on the Isonzo front in the north-east of Italy.

As the French contributed far more troops to the Western Front, and much of the fighting was taking place on their territory—the war never once extended into Germany itself—Haig did not have the final say over the grand strategy and timing of campaigns and attacks; moreover he was under direct instructions from the British government 'to assist the French and Belgian governments in driving the German armies from Belgian and French territory'.[15] His duty was therefore to fit in with French commander-in-chief Joseph Joffre's overall plans. But where to attack? In 1916 the BEF's five armies numbered fifty-six infantry and five cavalry divisions, a total of 1.4 million troops.[16] As soon as Haig took over in December 1915, he ordered his staff to plan for another major offensive at Ypres in Flanders, to the north of the Somme sector. It was Joffre who persuaded him to attack at the Somme instead. (In a sense 'The Somme' is a misnomer for the battle, because no British soldier saw action anywhere near the river, and few even so much as laid eyes on it as it was not even in the British sector.)

It was important that there should be a major Anglo-French offensive on the Western Front in mid-1916 so that it could form part of a massive, coordinated, continent-wide plan to defeat the

Central Powers. The middle of the year would see a simultaneous attack on all fronts against Germany and Austria-Hungary,
pushing them to their limit strategically and it was hoped preventing them from shifting reserves and resources from one
front to another. The Allied leaders met at Chantilly in France
in December 1915 and agreed a strategy of attack with France,
Britain, Italy and Russia acting together.[17] The attack on the
Somme would be co-ordinated with a Russian attack against
the Austro-Hungarians (the Brusilov Offensive[*]), which would
encourage the entry of Romania into the war on the Allies' side,
and a major Italian offensive against Austria on the plateau of
the Carso above the river Isonzo. Victories in each theatre would
leave the Central Powers surrounded on every side.

Political considerations ought to play a minimal part in the
formulation of strategy, though of course wars are ultimately
fought for political reasons. The decision to attack on the
Somme was in large part a political one, however, as it was the
theatre of war where the French and British armies were adja-
cent to one another, so they could conduct operations jointly,
the entente in action. Furthermore, if the Allies were to break
through decisively, the Somme seemed like a good place to do
so. The area north of Ypres was wet and prone to flooding; south
of Verdun there were rivers, forests and mountains; between
the two sectors the rivers Oise and Aisne ran through relatively
steep valleys. What was ideally needed were gently undulating,
dry chalky slopes with the minimum of forest, where cavalry
could operate and where the railways ran on an east–west axis.[18]

---

[*] Named after the Russian commander in the south-western sector, Gen. Alexei
Brusilov.

Artois and the Champagne district offered these apparently perfect conditions, but the Allied offensives there had ended in the painful Battles of Loos and Vimy Ridge. Now it was time for the Somme—a chalk plateau overlaid with loamy soil and cut by small ravines—to come into its own.

Detailed Staff discussions for a joint Anglo-French attack on the Somme had started in December 1915, immediately following the Chantilly conference, and by early 1916 it was agreed that an offensive would take place in mid-April, though only a minor one intended to thin out the German reserves there.[19] Haig wanted to delay the main attack so that it would coincide with the Italian and Russian offensives later in the summer. At a meeting on 20 January, Joffre agreed that the major British offensive of the summer could be in Flanders, so long as there was also a major attack on the Somme in the spring, and then on 14 February Haig and Joffre agreed that the BEF would attack on the Somme in early July.

The French Gen. (later Maréchal) Ferdinand Foch meanwhile did not want to fight on a wide front on the Somme, believing there were not enough heavy guns on the Allied side; he wanted to attack in one concentrated area.[20] Joffre overruled him, demanding co-ordinated assaults across the largest possible area. Haig had a low opinion of Foch, whom he thought of as a mere military theorist, and agreed with Joffre, though their expectations from the Somme Offensive proved to be wildly divergent. By mid-February 1916, the planned operation had ballooned to one that would involve no fewer than forty French and twenty-five British divisions. It was intended to start on 1 July. Gen. Erich von Falkenhayn's massive attack on the French at Verdun on

GENERAL JOSEPH JOFFRE
*The French general privately thought that Haig's hope for a breakthrough
was unachievable, and that the war would be won by attrition.*

21 February 1916 altered all their plans and strategic thinking. This made an early, large-scale Somme offensive all the more necessary, in Richard Holmes' phrase, in order to 'drag the Germans from the French windpipe at Verdun'.[21] That windpipe was the Voie Sacrée (Sacred Road) from Verdun to Bar-le-Duc, which could only be saved if German attention was directed elsewhere.[22] Only six weeks after the Battle of Verdun began, France had suffered no fewer than 90,000 casualties.[23]

When Joffre visited Haig at his HQ in May, French losses at Verdun were expected to be 200,000 by the end of the month. When Haig promised an attack in the Somme area between 1 July and 15 August, Joffre said that 'the French army would cease to exist'[24] if the latter date was chosen. Haig therefore promised Saturday, 1 July as the day that twelve British divisions would attack north of the Somme, and Joffre promised that twenty French formations would attack south of the river. The date was thus set, although the size of the various forces changed later. Those six weeks would probably have made little difference to the outcome, but when added to the other alterations in British plans demanded by Joffre, Haig's options were drastically narrowed. His later defenders have much right on their side when they point out how constrained he was. As Corelli Barnett has written: 'It was in no way Haig's fault that he had to launch his half-trained rank-and-file led by ill-experienced commanders in a premature offensive against immensely strong defences manned by the best army in Europe.'[25]

Haig himself had high hopes that after a massive bombardment on the Somme, his troops would be able simply to occupy the trenches of a demoralized enemy and then pursue the

GENERAL ERICH VON FALKENHAYN
*Pictured left, with his Chief of Staff Colonel Hans Hesse, he completely
disrupted the Allies' plans with his massive attack on Verdun.*

breakthrough he had wanted for so long. By contrast, Joffre had
privately concluded that Haig's hope for a breakthrough was a
chimera, and that the war would instead be won by attrition—
usure—which of course would necessitate far larger loss of life,
French and British as well as German.[26] One might—perhaps
morally one should—deplore the heinous cynicism of trying to
win a war by bleeding the enemy white at a terrible cost to one's
own countrymen, but at least Joffre could excuse himself on the

basis that he was ultimately proved right, and that no one else had any better ideas.[27]

The German strategy on the Somme in 1916, meanwhile, was entirely defensive while their armies in the east, supported by the Austro-Hungarians and the Turks, tried to knock Russia out of the war, which would allow them to bring their full weight to bear on the Western Front. The surprise Verdun Offensive was intended to kill as many Frenchmen as possible, relying on French pride in not withdrawing from the iconic fortress city on the Meuse, and it was largely successful in this. There was no need for Germany to advance on the Somme, even if they had the capacity to do so, which they did not during the Verdun Offensive. For over a year the Germans had therefore been digging deep dugouts and laying out barbed wire across the whole front. The Prussians and Bavarians they stationed there were not the hardened, experienced veterans of legend; because the sector had been hitherto so quiet, units were sent there for rest, recuperation and time in the reserves. Many came from the south of Germany and tended to despise the Prussians, and had only joined up after war broke out. The troops were mostly in reserve regiments not officered by career soldiers. 'They were the sorts of soldiers who defined the German army of the middle war years,' writes an historian of the Central Powers, 'grumbling about rations, praying to God to protect them just that little bit longer, and yearning for Maria, Ursel or Greta. It was their bad fortune to be in the path of a juggernaut determined, as they saw it, to carry the devastation around them into their homeland.'[28]

By the spring of 1916 the French army seemed to be suffering far more than its German opponent, because of its heroic but bloodily expensive stubbornness in refusing to yield up Verdun. (As with the Russians at Stalingrad in the Second World War, French honour was bound up in this symbolic citadel, which was the centre of a vast network of forts and bunkers.) The British Secretary of State for War, Lord Kitchener, had not wanted the BEF to shoulder the main weight of fighting the Germans in 1916, preferring a policy of 'defensive attrition' until the army was properly trained and equipped.[29] On 5 June, however, he was drowned in HMS *Hampshire* west of the Orkney Islands on his way to Russia, so Haig was able to impose an ambitious battle plan that Kitchener had never envisaged nor wanted. The level of Haig's ambition may be judged by the widespread belief in the General Staff that the offensive would be the 'Big Push' that could indeed bring the war to a successful conclusion. Although Haig drew up plans that envisaged a great breakthrough, he had the political sense to try to minimize expectations in the event of failure. 'It is always well to disclaim great hopes before an attack,' he wrote to General Charteris, his chief of Intelligence, the day before the assault.[30]

The ground north of the river Somme that was about to be contested so aggressively had been fought over scores of times by almost every army that had invaded or made war in France over the centuries; indeed some of the same farms had been occupied by the Cossacks fighting Napoleon I in 1814 and by Bavarians fighting his nephew Napoleon III in 1870. The undulating, chalky Picardy farmland and the meandering Somme and Ancre Rivers formed a sector which was also pitted with small villages whose names meant nothing to the world before

1916 but were forever afterwards to be synonymous with untold slaughter. The Germans had been expecting and methodically preparing for an attack in the Somme sector, which had been quiet since September 1914. Some German divisions there had hardly lost a man since then.[31] The first two lines of German trenches—a third was under construction—had been built long before by Russian prisoners captured on the Eastern Front, and the 2nd Army of General Fritz von Below and the 6th Army commanded by Crown Prince Rupprecht of Bavaria had had twenty-one months to perfect their defences.[32] The German Staff had analyzed the war's previous battles carefully, and

CROWN PRINCE
RUPPRECHT OF
BAVARIA
*Promoted to
Field Marshal shortly
after the first day of
the Somme Offensive,
Prince Rupprecht
was one of the few
royal officers considered
worthy of his command
in the German army.
He was a decent man,
competent commander
and future anti-
Nazi.*

ordered the construction of deep dugouts, protected bunkers, solid strongpoints and well-hidden forward operation posts, and they had thought especially carefully about their machine guns' fields of fire. They also kept modifying their plans as new information became available.[33] The more advanced dugouts had several exits and were sophisticated enough to incorporate kitchens and supply rooms for food, ammunition and equipment such as grenades, ammunition and woollen socks. Some even had rails attached to the steps so that machine guns could be pulled up quickly and placed into position on the parapet.[34]

Although Haig would have preferred to attack at Ypres, he took solace from the fact that the Somme had better railway access and drier ground.[35] The chalk downlands of Picardy have roughly the same geology as Kent, yet that very similarity made it relatively easy for the Germans to dig deeply into the ground.* Whatever advantages lay with the BEF and French as the attackers, they were heavily outweighed by the disadvantages. The Germans had been in possession of the area since the early weeks of the war, and they held almost all the high ground along the battlefront, especially at Beaumont Hamel, the Schwaben Redoubt north of the village of Thiepval, and Thiepval itself, making the tasks of their machine-gunners and artillery forward observation officers very much easier. There were no fewer than eleven redoubts in the sector, as well as the nine fortified towns.

Walking today from the magnificent, Edwin Lutyens-designed Thiepval Memorial to the Missing out to the Leipzig

---

* The trench lines are easily discernible from the air today as white lines in the fields.

Redoubt, one can see the panoramic view of the British lines that the German machine-gunners on the ridge enjoyed on 1 July 1916. In a terrain of fields and small woods on undulating slopes, the long chalk ridge runs from Thiepval to Morval with the village of Pozières at its highest point. There is a straight Roman road from Albert (which was behind the British front line) to Bapaume (which was behind the German positions). The German forward posts tended to be on the leading edge of the ridge, which included the highly fortified, stone-built villages of (from north to south) Serre, Beaumont Hamel, Thiepval, Ovillers, La Boisselle, Fricourt, Mametz and Curlu, many of whose houses were built over deep and protective cellars.

Maj. Richard Spencer Smith, second-in-command of the 2nd Battalion Hampshire Regiment, ably summed up the immense strength of the German defences:

> For defensive purposes the siting of the German trenches could hardly have been better. It possessed the following advantages:
>
> 1 Front line system almost immune from high velocity shellfire owing to configuration of the ground;
> 2 Irregularity of design, making exact ranging difficult and minor salient… giving opportunity for crossfire of machine guns from well concealed positions. And concealments for redoubts and strongpoints;
> 3 Excellent natural cover for supports and reserves and immunity from shellfire in caves, cellars and dugouts;
> 4 Covered communications immune from shellfire;
> 5 The Germans had good observation from high ground… opposite Thiepval;

6　The trench system was protected by very strong wire entanglements; the British had to advance over a crest line making a splendid target for artillery and machine guns.[36]

The Germans had undoubtedly used their time well in constructing the strongest position on the Western Front.[37] With dugouts linked by buried telephone cables and with deep communications trenches, hidden machine gun posts offering wide fields of fire across treeless fields, dense thickets of barbed wire several feet deep and up to 5 feet (1.5 m) high, it was a formidable obstacle.

However, after visiting the Somme sector in February 1916, Gen. Sir Henry 'Rawly' Rawlinson, commander of the BEF's 4th Army, had been encouraged to see the German positions on the forward slopes of the ridge, thinking this meant that they could be bombarded with greater accuracy than if they had been sheltered behind the crest. He called it 'capital country in which to undertake an offensive... for the observation is excellent and with plenty of guns and ammunition we ought to be able to avoid the heavy losses which the infantry have always suffered on previous occasions'.[38] Yet for all their vulnerablity, the forward slope positions also gave the Germans superb visibility over the ground across which the British and French would have to advance.

When the 4th Army arrived to prepare for the battle from the north in March 1916, its formations found that the trenches held by the 3rd Army since the summer of 1915 had been well kept and laid out properly. There were fire trenches with traverses, preventing an attacker firing down the whole length of a front-line trench; support trenches two hundred yards (182.8 m) or so behind the forward entrenchments; reserve trenches a further two hundred yards behind the supports; detailed trench maps, well-defined parapets and firing-steps, latrines and dugouts, though no shelters as sophisticated or deep as the German equivalents.[39]

The brigades of the 4th Army typically rotated each of their four battalions through the front line and the reserve trenches and then sent them for rest and recuperation behind the lines every sixteen days, and they had only had three months in their new posts before the great offensive began.[40] They settled in quickly, and indulged in the British Tommies' traditional penchant for anglicizing French names, so that Mouquet Ferme became Mucky Farm, Auchonvillers became Ocean Villas, and it requires little imagination to guess what the soldiers called Assevillers and Fouquevillers.* Other place names invented by the British army on the Somme, sometimes on the flimsiest of pretexts, included Caterpillar Valley, Wellington Redoubt, Shrine Alley, Casino Point, Bottom Wood, Bucket Trench, Strip Trench, Crucifix Trench, Quadrangle Trench, Pearl Alley, Acid Drop Copse, Beetle Alley, Willow Avenue, Lozenge Wood, The Dingle, Wine Street, Paradise Alley, Sandbag Corner and Salop Avenue.[41]

The men made the best they could of trench life, where the atmosphere was claustrophobic and one had to crouch for much of the time in order not to offer a target to snipers. Lice infestations were sometimes found even in the 'clean' clothing that was issued to the men. One of the reasons that officers' terriers were

---

* Elsewhere in the war, the British Army's phonetics turned Ypres into 'Wipers', Ploegsteert into 'Plug Street' and Étaples into 'Eetaps'.

popular in the trenches was that there were rats 'the size of cats' in the trenches and in no man's land, which fed off the corpses (as did carrion crows and flies). Trenches were commonly between six feet (1.8 m) and six foot six inches (2 m) deep, and provided protection (except from the dreaded mortar fire) for British soldiers who averaged five foot six inches (1.68 m) in height. They needed a firing-step from which to shoot at the enemy, and often had foliage or wicker on top to break up their outlines against sniper fire.* Trenches were shaped in a continuous zig-zag pattern so as to absorb blast waves in the event of a successful mortar hit, and to prevent enfilading fire in the event of the Germans capturing a trench.

Trenches came in five types: a 'front' or 'fire' trench was out in the most exposed position, with a 'support' trench behind it and a 'reserve' trench behind that. A 'communication' trench ran between them. The 'assembly' trenches, from where attacks were launched, were usually the fire trenches. Sometimes a new assembly trench might be built if the German artillery had already found the range of the fire trench.

The best novel to be published about the first day of the Somme is *Covenant with Death*, by John Harris. Published in 1961, the same year in which Alan Clark's denunciation of Haig appeared, it captures the effects on his family of the battle, in which his father and father-in-law fought in the Sheffield City Battalion without injury, his brother-in-law and an uncle were gassed, two other uncles lost their legs and a fourth was killed. Harris

---

* The term sniper dated from the eighteenth century, and referred to the accuracy needed for shooting snipe.

records vividly the down-to-earth flavour of the average soldier's outlook on the war, interpreting the high-flown rhetoric of politicians, clergymen and newspapers: '*Entente Cordiale?* "Our lot" to everybody else. *Noble Allies?* "Froggies" was good enough for most of us. *Prussian militarists?* "Kaiser Bill" to the troops.'[42] It was a citizen army that fought on the Somme: over half of the 120,000 infantrymen who attacked on the first day were volunteers. Almost half of the divisions—eight of the seventeen—were made up of four Regular Army and four Territorial divisions. Although conscription had been introduced in January 1916, those men were still in training and so were not present on the Somme.

Between August 1914 and December 1915, some 2,466,719 men enlisted in what became known as Kitchener's New Army,* comprising 43 per cent of the 5.7 million men who served during the war. It was the second-largest volunteer force in history, after the Indian army of 1939–45.[43] Many of them joined up in response to appeals for manpower made by Earl Kitchener, the most famous of which was of course the recruitment poster featuring his face and pointing finger. 'There wasn't even any point in drawing whiskers on it', John Harris wrote of that poster, 'because it already had a better set than anybody could have added on with a pencil. There was something about it that made it personal enough for a man to look over his shoulder, "YOUR KING AND COUNTRY NEED YOU", it seemed to say, not HIM. Nor *him*. Not the clerk on his way home, arguing about the price of plums over the barrow by the arches. Not the miner in the flat

---

* Or, colloquially, 'Kitchener's Mob'.

cap round the corner with his face in a pint pot. YOU. And you felt a little prouder for having answered.'[44]

The immediate response had swamped the War Office's capacity to equip the New Army, so early training was undertaken in the volunteers' own clothes and shoes before proper uniforms were ready. The men were enthusiastic and sang sentimental, unmilitary songs on the march such as 'Tipperary', 'Long Long Trail', 'Keep the Home Fires Burning' and 'If You Were the Only Girl in the World'. Only later on did they sing the sardonic, almost anti-war song 'We're Here Because We're Here', to the tune of 'Auld Lang Syne'. Yet although it became fashionable to argue that these men were mere sheep led to the slaughter who did not really know what they were fighting for, that is untrue. They might not have made much of the reasons for their service, in the way that soldiers rarely do, but they well knew that they were fighting to save Civilization in general and the British empire in particular from Prussian militarist tyranny. Many of the letters the soldiers wrote home, and the inscriptions some parents chose for their sons' headstones, spoke of the necessity of the sacrifice in order to keep Britain and Europe free.

The first battalions of Kitchener's New Army were assembled in the autumn of 1914 and deployed by the end of 1915. The idea for having what came to be called 'Pals' battalions has been ascribed to Gen. Sir Henry 'Rawly' Rawlinson, who wanted soldiers to be recruited into battalions together from people in the same trades, and from the same backgrounds, social clubs, places of work, church groups and so on, because it was thought that friendship and community of interest would be good for

GENERAL SIR HENRY RAWLINSON

Sir Henry 'Rawly' Rawlinson, commander of the BEF's 4th Army at the Somme,
pictured here on the steps of his headquarters at Querrieu Chateau, July 1916.

regimental cohesiveness and pride. So the 10th Battalion Royal
Fusiliers was the 'Stockbrokers' Battalion', for example, the
8th Battalion London Regiment was the 'Post Office Rifles', the
15th Battalion London Regiment was the 'Civil Service Rifles',
and there were also 'Football', 'Sportsmen' and 'Public Works'
battalions. The names of these locally recruited 'Pals' battalions such as London Scottish, London Irish, Tyneside Scottish
and Tyneside Irish reflected proud ethnic backgrounds. Units
such as the 'Public Schools Battalion', 'Artists' Rifles', 'North
Eastern Railway Pioneers', 'Grimsby Chums' (The 10th Lincolns), 'Belfast Young Citizens' (14th Royal Irish Rifles), 'Leeds
Pals' (15th West Yorkshires) and so on also promoted strong

regimental morale. Yet they were not the complete green-horns of popular myth; they had generally been training for nine months in Britain and a further nine to twelve in France or Flanders learning the particular complexities of the Western Front before they ever set foot in a forward trench. Most units had lived in the trenches and conducted trench raids and suffered casualties before 1 July 1916.

Morale was generally extremely high. Entirely typical is this account from Pte. Arthur Edwin Wrench of the 5th Battalion Seaforth Highlanders in the 51st (Highland) Division, who kept a diary from 1915 till 1919. In a preface written in Glasgow in 1921, he recalled how on his journey through France to the front:

> We stopped at several stations on the way where parties
> of ladies fed us with sandwiches, cakes and tea. Then as
> we started on our way, wet eyes, sad faces and waving
> handkerchiefs receded from us as we raised our battle-cry
> enthusiastically 'Are we downhearted? No!' Their tears
> were none of our business, for this adventure was far too
> thrilling and exciting, and I do believe now that each one
> of us, like every other soldier going to war for the first
> time, fondly imagined that this draft was on its way to deal
> the final and decisive blow, and achieve the last triumph.
> What a delusion… Yet through it all one's optimism
> emerged supreme and this was the thing that kept our
> spirits alive and the souls burning within us as we tried to
> keep our faith with those at home who trusted in us and
> upon whose promises we also relied.[45]

The BEF was divided into five armies, each of which was made up of between two and four corps. Each corps was commanded by a lieutenant-general and consisted of a number of infantry divisions, and could number up to 120,000 men. Each infantry division, commanded by a major-general, consisted of three infantry brigades and included up to 12,000 infantry as well as 2,000 Royal Engineers and pioneers, 3,500 artillerymen, 750 medical as well as supply staff, and could thus number 20,000 at full strength. At the time of the Battle of the Somme, an infantry brigade was composed of four infantry battalions, each with its engineer, signals, mortar, machine gun and ambulance units. Although each battalion, commanded by a lieutenant-colonel, was supposed to number around 1,100 men, very often after

THE GENERALS
General Officers of World War I (*1922*) *by John Singer Sargent.* Fifth from left: *Henry Rawlinson*; tenth from left: *Henry Wilson*; ninth, eighth and seventh from right: *Douglas Haig, John French and William Robertson.*

illness, wounds, leave and other factors diminished the unit, they could often actually field only around two-thirds of that number. Battalions had four companies of around 200 men commanded by a major or captain, which were divided into four platoons each commanded by a lieutenant, and these consisted of four sections commanded by a sergeant.[46]

The BEF's order of battle on the Somme on 1 July comprised two armies (the 3rd and 4th), six corps (III, VIII, X, XIII, XV and VII), and seventeen infantry divisions comprising fifty-one brigades. Every division had a pioneer battalion of fully trained

infantrymen who were also specialists in digging trenches, laying out barbed wire and all the other back-breaking labouring duties associated with trench warfare. As a general rule, the 1st and 2nd battalions of a regiment comprised its Regulars, the 3rd and 4th its Territorials, and the 5th onwards its Kitchener New Army volunteers. Those conscripted after January 1916 went into its service battalions.

The British army had expanded in the two years since the war broke out from 247,000 Regulars and 246,000 Territorials to 1.25 million men.[47] This meant that the officers who commanded corps of tens of thousands of men in 1916 were the same men who had only two years earlier been brigadiers commanding a fraction of that number. As the British army before 1914 was more of a colonial police force than a continental war-fighting force, their officers had little experience of corps and none of armies and there was very little opportunity to exercise field command above battalion or brigade level.[48] In 1914 there were fewer than 13,000 officers in the British army, but by 1918 there were 13,000 Staff officers, and over 25,000 officers in the Royal Regiment of Artillery alone.[49]

Considering how little experience the senior officers had, it would be unsurprising if they had been cautious, uninspiring and lacking in much optimism or confidence about how to win the war. Yet although Haig's High Command has indeed been accused of having limited vision, when it came to the plan of attack for 1 July 1916, the biggest problem was not the narrowness of its vision but its dangerous ambition.

TWO

TACTICS

'My strongest recollection:
all those grand looking cavalrymen, ready mounted
to follow the breakthrough. What a hope!'[1]

PTE. E. T. RADBAND,
5th West Yorkshire Regiment

*

'I made up my mind that, if ever I got out of it alive,
there wasn't enough gold in the Bank of England
to get me back again.'[2]

LCPL. J. A. HENDERSON,
Belfast Young Citizens' Battalion

Until the advent of the tank on the battlefield ten weeks after the opening of the Somme Offensive, there was no alternative in attack to sending men into no man's land* and trying to seize the enemy's front trench and kill or capture everyone in it. Yet at the Battle of Loos and in many other previous engagements of the war, this had proved prohibitively costly, and for one primary reason: the machine gun. In 1916 the German army's three independent machine gun companies were amalgamated into *Maschinengewehr-Scarfschützen-Abteilungen*. Each new division had no fewer than seventy-two heavy machine guns, increasing to 350 by 1918.

Although the concept of a multi-firing gun was almost as old as that of the musket itself, it took until the nineteenth century for a strong enough metal to be smelted that could withstand the pressure of sustained repeated firing, and for manufacturing processes to become capable of creating the necessary fractional tolerances for each part of such a complex weapon. In 1862 an inventor from North Carolina, Richard Gatling, produced a crank-operated gun capable of firing 200 rounds per minute. In 1888 Hiram Maxim, an inventor from Maine who settled in England, perfected a machine gun that continued to fire until the finger was taken off the trigger. Never in the field of human conflict could so many be killed so quickly by so few. The Maxim gun that wrought such havoc amongst the British infantry on

* 'No man's land' comes from early fourteenth-century English, meaning land, usually barren, over which nobody has established legal ownership.

1 July 1916 was a water-cooled, belt-fed 7.92 mm calibre weapon that weighed 57.3 lbs (26 kg) and could fire 500 rounds per minute at a 900 yard (823 m) per second muzzle velocity. Its optimum range was 2,000 yards (1,829 m) but it was still reasonably accurate at twice that distance. It could fit 250 rounds on each of the belts that fed the gun, and a new belt could be fitted in a matter of seconds. The French nicknamed it 'the lawnmower' or 'coffee-grinder', the English 'the Devil's paintbrush'.

The British perfected their Vickers machine gun too, of course. The memorial to the Machine Gun Corps of the First World War, which stands at the end of Park Lane on Hyde Park Corner in London, is of a naked 'Boy David' by the sculptor Francis Derwent Wood. Its inscription—'Saul hath slain his thousands, but David his tens of thousands'—might sound harshly insensitive to modern ears but did not at its unveiling in 1925, when it was recalled that over 62,000 of the 170,000-strong unit had been killed or wounded during the First World War, earning the corps the soubriquet 'The Suicide Club'.

In order to counter the Maxim gun, Gens Haig and Rawlinson devised a plan to use the huge Allied superiority in artillery in the Somme sector utterly to destroy the enemy front-line trenches. Haig was persuaded by the artillerymen on the staff at General Headquarters (GHQ) that a preliminary bombardment lasting five days was better than a short surprise barrage just before the attack, as it would drive the Germans into their dugouts and destroy them there.[3] After so many hours of intense and incessant bombardment, it was believed that the British infantry would then only need to advance at walking pace to occupy the trenches after the artillery fire 'lifted' from the front

AN 18-POUNDER IN ACTION
The standard British field gun of the war: of the some fifteen million shells fired
during the Battle of the Somme, roughly ten million were fired by 18-pounders.

line onto the support line. They would make prisoners of any demoralized Germans who might still be alive, and then move on forward deeper into the enemy positions. That at least was the plan.

While Allenby's 3rd Army created a diversion around Gommecourt, Rawlinson's 4th Army would capture German positions across the 27,000 yards (24,689 m) between Serre and Montauban, with the French 6th Army pushing on to Curlu further south. After that the 4th Army would take the German second-line positions from the river Ancre to Pozières, after beating back any German counter-attacks. They were so certain the bombardment would work that they modified the 'fire and movement' form of attack with new tactical instructions.

Training Divisions for Offensive Action (SS 109) and *Tactical Notes* now ordered: 'The assaulting troops must push forward at a steady pace in successive lines, each line adding fresh impetus to the preceding line.'[4]

Haig devolved the writing of the overall battle plan to Rawlinson, whose overall tactical objective has been summed up in the phrase 'bite and hold', whereby the infantry would seize a small amount of ground and then hold it against the inevitable German counter-attack.[5]* Rawlinson's preferred attack would be cautious and only undertaken after a bombardment that concentrated on the German front-line positions rather than including the second and third lines behind them. When Haig saw these plans in early April, however, he thought them over-prudent, believing that the sheer weight of the bombardment they were preparing would allow the infantry to reach the German second line of defences north of Pozières, and in the south further than that, up to a distance of 5,000 yards (4,572 m). Haig's optimistic mood persisted, and by June his intention for the attack was 'to break the enemy's defensive system'. He therefore demanded that the plan be changed to include a much deeper penetration of the German lines eastwards, to 2,500 yards (2,286 m), or over 1.4 miles (2.25 km), in the north and centre of the battlefield, incorporating the enemy's second-line positions and in some cases even beyond them.[6] By extending the attack to the second and sometimes third lines of German trenches, however, Haig asked for more than his 1,010 field guns and howitzers,

---

* As an undergraduate at the University of Cambridge in the 1980s, I was taught never to state that anything is ever inevitable in history, as it cannot be. That is of course true, *except* in the case of German counter-attack.

427 medium and heavy guns and howitzers, and 100 support-ing French guns and howitzers could deliver. (To oppose these, Germany had 454 light guns, 372 field guns and 18 heavy guns.)[7]

Whereas Haig saw capturing the Thiepval-Morval Ridge as the start of a larger, wider campaign to break through into the open countryside beyond the German lines, Rawlinson wanted to stop there, and deal with German counter-attacks by their reserve divisions. Originally, Rawlinson had wanted to move 1,250 yards (1,143 m) (nearly three-quarters of a mile (1.2 km)) into the German first defensive line north of the Ancre, halting at Beaucourt Ridge, where they could be supported by artillery. His intention was 'to kill as many Germans as possible with the least loss to ourselves', and this, as one historian has remarked, was more important to him at that moment than seizing ground he was doubtful of being able to hold.[8] When Rawlinson was forced to redraw his plan, he gave no indication that he had changed his mind.

It was not good that the commander-in-chief and his chief planner did not agree about the fundamental objectives of such a vital offensive, and Rawlinson's chief staff officer later wrote: 'I admit at once the objectives were too deep and too broad for the troops and guns available.'[9] When Haig radically altered the plan, Rawlinson noted: 'D. H. is for breaking the line and gam-bling on rushing the 3rd line on the top of a [German] panic.'[10] Haig's objective was the high ground of the Pozières Ridge across 10 miles (16 km), and once taken the BEF would turn north, enfilading along the German line. The cavalry would cap-ture Bapaume and strike deep into the country behind the lines, with the French protecting the south.[11] Haig liked and trusted

Rawlinson personally, but he was also a strong-willed, highly political soldier while Haig was the commander-in-chief. Rawlinson had little way of gainsaying him even had he so desired.

Of course in retrospect it is easy to see that this battle plan was wildly over-ambitious. The case for the prosecution was put memorably by Basil Liddell Hart. In 1938 he wrote :

> Haig gambled on a complete break-through. His justifi-
> cation is not easy to discover. For, even by the standards
> and experience of 1915, he was deficient of the means for
> such an ambitious plan. Only heavy guns could smash the
> German defences. Only surprise could open a passage
> quickly, and keep it open long enough for his reserves to
> sweep through to Bapaume into open country... yet he
> had far fewer heavy guns than the French alongside him,
> for a far wider frontage than theirs, and his plan forswore
> any real attempt at surprise.[12]

But Haig's plan at least had the attribute of not relying on mere attrition to win the war, on the grinding, seemingly endless tit-for-tat mutual slaughter for which both sides were to settle until almost the final hundred days up to November 1918. These were not, in fact, the unimaginative, murderous, almost criminal tactics of which Haig has so often been accused. The problem was that they were too imaginative, wishing to circumvent the pounding attritional warfare that was costing so many lives. Yet the final plan was something of a compromise between the Haig and Rawlinson versions. Haig wanted a much shorter, more intense bombardment, a breakthrough with strong patrols rather than waves of men marching in line abreast, and cavalry exploitation of any breakthroughs achieved.[13] Under his revision of the plan, the BEF attacked with thirteen divisions (with four in reserve), while the French attacked with five (with six in reserve). Against these twenty-eight divisions, the Germans had a mere five, with two in reserve. The Allies thus had far greater numerical superiority in the Somme Offensive, which at least on paper should have guaranteed victory. They also enjoyed air superiority, having 386 aircraft versus Germany's 128.[14] This should have given the Allies nearly complete control of the skies above the battlefield, and the ability to detect the positions of German artillery as well as spotting the fall of their own gunners' shells.[15]

On 16 and 21 June, the 4th Army received orders from GHQ about how the cavalry should exploit a breakthrough, showing Haig's optimism about the coming attack. Some historians, such as Gary Sheffield, believe that the very existence of this contingency plan proves he was wholly unprepared for the battle of attrition he was shortly to experience, but although he has been castigated for believing that cavalry could play any role in a modern war, in fact it did have a strictly limited one, and Haig was correct to factor it into his plans, although of course he never envisaged situations where horses would charge into machine gun fire. Haig never managed to employ cavalry en masse in the way he would have liked, but that does not mean that he was stupid to plan to use it. His post-war speech on the importance of the 'well-bred horse' on the battlefield was wrenched out of

THE DECCAN HORSE LINE-UP (OVERLEAF)
*The Indian cavalry regiment wait for the order to advance
during the Battle of Bazentin Ridge, 14 July 1916. Later that day,
they took part in the last cavalry charge of the war.*

context by the military historian Basil Liddell Hart further to damage Haig's reputation, yet when it is read in full it reveals itself to be anything but the ravings of a dinosaur and is instead a moderately progressive statement of all-arms tactics as they were understood at the time. In an era before widespread mechanization, horses could move cavalrymen quickly—and Haig also wanted to use them as mounted infantry—around the rear and flanks of the battlefield. (Mobility was a real problem for commanders of this era; the French had famously been forced to use taxis at the Battle of the Marne.) The idea of retaining a cavalry corps in reserve in the hope of a breakthrough makes sense when one considers that tanks had not yet been used, went at 2 mph (3.2 kmph) at the beginning of the war (and only 8 mph (12.9 kmph) by 1918 and often broke down. Cavalry was used to exploit German weaknesses in August 1918, although by then it made up only 3 per cent of total army manpower.

Although Joffre rather than Haig was responsible for where and when the attack was to take place, the British commander-in-chief must take overall responsibility for how that attack developed on the battlefield. At Verdun, Falkenhayn had attacked across an 8-mile (12.8 km) sector, which was narrow enough to leave his infantry exposed to enfilading fire from French guns on either wing. To avoid a similar fate Haig decided to attack along an enormous 18 miles (29 km) of front.[16] The British infantry would come at a right angle eastwards towards Gommecourt, Beaumont Hamel, Thiepval, Ovillers and La Boisselle, and northwards towards Fricourt, Mametz and Montauban. Yet this had the effect of spreading out the artillery's targets too thinly. 'His feeling was that if he was prepared for a breakthrough if the opportunity presented itself, he could then take full advantage of it,' his widow Countess Haig wrote after the war, 'but if a breakthrough was not achieved then no harm would be done. He did not want another Loos.'[17] As with so many of Lady Haig's remarks, the unfortunate phrase 'no harm would be done' in relation to the first day of the Somme would not redound to her late husband's credit. Although it is true that in the early planning stages Haig was more optimistic than Rawlinson, by late May he had become cautious, and stressed to Rawlinson the importance of establishing a good position for the 1917 campaign.[18] In his diary for 15 June, Haig wrote '<u>If [the] Enemy's defence is strong</u> and fighting continues for many days, as soon as the Pozières heights are gained, the position should be consolidated, and improved.'[19]

A great deal was asked of individual units in the battle plan. It called for the 36th (Ulster) Division, for example, to gain over 3,000 yards (2,743 m) by 10.08 a.m., the very exactitude of the timing showing how little the General Staff took notice of FM Helmuth von Moltke's classic dictum that 'No plan survives first contact with the enemy.' There was far too much organization and inflexibility; everything was arranged with minute attention to detail, especially the lifting barrage that in fact moved on far faster and further than the infantry it was supposed to support. The battle plan for VIII Corps alone, for example, was seventy-six pages long, with a 365-page supplement at divisional level.[20] 'There must be a colossal lack of organization somewhere', the future poet laureate, Cecil Day-Lewis, wrote in his Royal Flying Corps logbook, having seen the offensive develop from the air, but in fact there was too much organization.[21]

Part of the explanation for this obsessive micro-managing by the General Staff can be put down to Haig and Rawlinson's doubts about how the Kitchener's New Army recruits would behave when they came under fire. They were uncertain about the steadiness of the volunteers when they finally went over the top. 'I have not got an Army in France, really,' Haig wrote in his diary as late as 29 March 1916, 'but a collection of divisions untrained for the field.'[22] On another occasion he wrote: 'Unless successful raids are made, troops cannot be depended upon in the general attack.'[23] This serious (if unfounded) concern led to the tactic of arranging the men in long lines across the battle-front, rather than in formations that made them less easy targets for the enemy's machine-gunners. 'The attack must be made in waves', Rawlinson told a friend just beforehand, 'with men at fairly close interval in order to give them confidence.'[24] Yet the men had the necessary confidence in themselves and their courage under fire, and they were proved right during the attack. It was the generals who lacked confidence in them.

Haig and Rawlinson did not expect the infantry to have to fight particularly hard for the trenches, but merely to occupy and rebuild them after they had been destroyed by the artillery, so they were given huge amounts of equipment which loaded them down as they crossed no man's land. The shovels they were carrying, for example, were for restoring the captured trenches and for burying dead Germans. Rawlinson's view was affected by the Battle of Neuve Chapelle in March 1915, after which he wrote that 'It is always possible by careful preparation and adequate artillery support by heavy Howitzers to pierce the enemy's line', assuming that field guns were capable of cutting barbed wire defences.[25] Yet at Neuve Chappelle there had been a gun for every 6 yards (5.4 m) of front, whereas on the Somme the 4th Army had 20,000 yards (18,288 m) of front, and only 245 heavy howitzers to cover it, a heavy gun to cover every 80 yards (73 m). The battle plan simply did not allocate the necessary amount of high explosive (HE) for Haig's far more ambitious ideas: under the new plan the preliminary bombardment would only use one pound (0.45 kg) of HE for every 10 square yards (8.36 sq. m), which, astonishing though it might seem, was to be nothing like enough.[26]

A serious problem for Haig's High Command throughout this planning period was a tendency towards over-optimistic 'group-think', a dangerous trait amongst military planners. Haig's Intelligence chief, Brig.-Gen. John Charteris, was a fellow Scot he had brought with him from India to his Aldershot command. His assessments tended to be consistently over-confident, yet Haig did not dismiss him until 1918, once Charteris had fallen out with the politically influential Secretary of State for War, the Earl of Derby. In May 1916, for example, Charteris underes-timated the capacities of the German divisions in his briefing of Haig regarding the enemy's reserves, on the basis that they were 'exhausted as a result of fighting at Verdun', not taking into account the fact that some of them were nonetheless capable, once reinforced, of fighting hard.[27] A recent historian of GHQ's

TOMMY'S EQUIPMENT (OVERLEAF)
The British infantryman carried an average of 66 lb (30 kg) into battle, drastically slowing him down in no man's land.

IN HAVERSACK: IN POCKETS: IN KNAPSACK: ON PERSON: AND EQUIPM

The burden borne so cheerfully by the British soldier on active service is not light; but it makes for efficiency and for comfort, which are everything. All the winter goat-skin coat, sundry comforts from home and other personal belongings, and, in some cases, extra rations and fuel. It has

IN KNAPSACK

ON PERSON

BURDEN CARRIED BY "TOMMY" WHEN MARCHING TO THE TRENCHES.

normally are illustrated above. They include everything each man carries when marching up to the trenches. In addition to the items dealt with may be added the very evident truth, that the British soldier is the best-equipped, and, it might be added, the best-fed fighting-man in the world.

Intelligence operation has suggested that there was 'an almost unconscious process whereby Charteris moulded his assessments to fit in with what he believed were Haig's opinions', although this did not became fully apparent until March 1917.[28] Yet if it had been going on at the time of the planning for the Somme—and Charteris owed his position entirely to Haig's patronage—it would have been a classic example of Intelligence serving rather than directing a general's thought patterns, and Charteris telling Haig what Haig wanted to hear, with disastrous consequences.

Another problem with Intelligence at the time was that although aerial photography could show enemy trenches and even individual dugouts, it could not discern how strongly the lines were held. Cavalry could no longer carry out reconnaissance in the age of trench warfare, so aeroplanes had to do the job, as well as help find enemy guns and help guide fire against them. In 1915 aerial photography and ground-to-air communications were invented, revolutionizing the efficacy of the air arm. In February 1916 at Verdun, fighter aircraft were employed by both sides to protect photo-reconnaissance planes, and of course to shoot down enemy observers. Haig liked and trusted Maj.-Gen. Hugh 'Boom' Trenchard, commander of the Royal Flying Corps (RFC), and supported his aggressive air strategy. His airmen paid a heavy price on the Somme, however: from 1 July to the end of the battle on 18 November the RFC lost 782 aircraft and 576 pilots.[29]

Other classic sources of intelligence were similarly limited; civilians were moved out of the combat areas, prisoners were hard to capture, newspapers were censored. So trench raids, sometimes with diversions, were staged to bring back information. The evidence collected in them could be as slight as a canteen cover with a regimental number stenciled onto it, but of course documents, orders, letters and prisoners were far better. In the days before the Somme Offensive, however, only about twenty prisoners were taken by the 4th Army because of the bombardment, not enough to deduce anything very useful. 'Although the raiders did not succeed in entering the enemy's trenches,' one regimental war diary noted, 'the Corps Commander considered that they attained most useful results, as it has been established that the enemy's front-line trenches are strongly held.'[30] Part of the reason why the British High Command believed so implicitly that the bombardment would destroy the German defences, barbed wire and morale was because General Joffre had said that that was the effect the German bombardment had had on the defenders of Verdun.[31] German prisoners captured on the Somme seemed to indicate that their morale had been broken. But the prisoners—even supposing they were telling the truth rather than what they thought their captors wanted to hear—were an unrepresentative group. They had been captured, after all.

There was thus a collective assumption, especially in VIII Corps, that the preliminary bombardment, and especially its final sixty-five minutes, would destroy and demoralize the Germans in their forward positions, yet intelligence contradicting that theory was gleaned throughout the previous week by trench raiders who found uncut wire, or were vigorously repulsed, which should have given planners pause for thought. 'Critical evaluation of the intelligence gathered over the previous seven days', one historian states, 'seems to have been non-existent.'[32] Here was group-think at its most pernicious.

It was not until 1917 and 1918 that aerial photography and signals intelligence provided much help to Charteris and his successors in trying to work out the whereabouts of German theatre reserves. The agent network in Belgium did not provide anything useful until 1917 either, and the situation was not helped by a turf war between GHQ's Intelligence operation and the Secret Intelligence Service.[33] The Allies had no moles in the German High Command or the senior reaches of government and had access to nothing like the Ultra decrypts that led to such brilliant results in the Second World War. Charteris was perhaps doing his best in very difficult circumstances, but if he was often flying blind it seems he did not confess his relative ignorance to his commander-in-chief. Few Intelligence chiefs ever do.

The surprising thing is that the general paucity of information induced such over-confidence in Charteris. In February 1917 he was still warning audiences, for example, not to believe that the enemy was in good shape, whereas in fact the German army really was a formidable machine almost up to the moment when it cracked in the summer of 1918. Charteris must not be used as a scapegoat for all the High Command's errors, however; every commander needs to be aware of the limitations of Intelligence. Besides, as the government insider Lord Esher told Haig's private secretary, Philip Sassoon, Charteris 'had no more *real* influence with Haig than his chauffeur'.[34]

By April 1916, British Intelligence had recognized that the Germans had improved their front-line defences on the Somme,

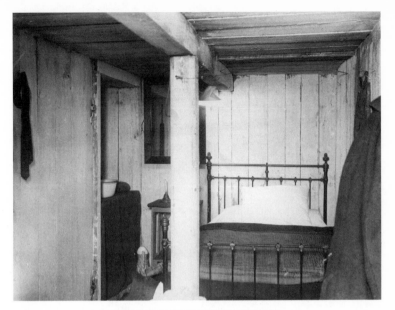

GERMAN UNDERGROUND DUGOUT
German trenches on the Somme tended to be considerably more comfortable—and better furnished—than Allied ones.

having long perfected their first and second lines and now starting on a third. Yet 4th Army planners did not know about the completion of the third line until the preliminary bombardment began.[35] They did know, and had since January, that the Germans were building significantly deeper dugouts and that the openings to these were placed at the front wall of the trenches rather than the back, making them harder for the artillery to hit.[36]

If Haig took the Intelligence material he received too much at face value, the soldiers in the field tended not to, believing that it was often false and occasionally absurdly esoteric. The corps Intelligence summary was nicknamed 'Comic Cuts', after a droll Victorian magazine, and the poet and writer 2nd Lt.

Siegfried Sassoon, attached to the 1st Battalion Royal Welch Fusiliers, part of 22nd Brigade of the 7th Division, recalled how on 27 June 1916 the Intelligence summary reported that a large number of enemy batteries had been silenced by British batteries (which he could tell they had not been) and that 'The anonymous humourist who compiled "Comic Cuts" was able to announce that the Russians had captured a redoubt and some heavy guns at Czartovijsk, which, he explained, was 44 miles (71 km) north-east of Luck.'[37]

By early April, British Intelligence knew that the Germans had four divisions in reserve behind their 6th Army, and by the end of May that this had increased to at least five because of British preparations at the Somme. After the Russians launched the Brusilov Offensive on 4 June and it became clear two weeks later how successful this attack had been, British Intelligence re-assessed the situation, based on agents' reports in Belgium about German troop movements eastwards. On 16 June Haig wrote in his diary that there was 'no doubt' that the enemy was taking troops away from his front and sending them to Russia, hence the reappearance of cavalry in his tactical thinking.[38] German records show that that there were ten divisions in the German reserve still on the Western Front on 1 July, of which six were facing the British sector and were in perfectly reasonable morale, while British Intelligence believed there were only three, of low morale.[39] Charteris wrote to his wife on 30 June, the day before the attack, 'We are fighting primarily to kill Germans and against their plans, [to] gain some valuable positions and generally prepare for the big offensive that must come sooner or later and if not this year then next.'[40] When he published his book *At GHQ*,[41] he altered the wording to read 'fighting primarily to wear down the German Armies and the German nation... and generally to prepare for the great decisive offensive'.[42] The veterans of the Somme were not told that all the bloodletting had been for such limited objectives as 'to prepare for the great decisive offensive'; many of them believed this was to be the actual great offensive.

Although the precise date of the 'Big Push' was not known outside the General Staff until just beforehand, nor its exact location, it was known in every pub in Britain that there was going to be a major offensive that summer. 'Everyone at home seemed to know that the long-planned offensive was due to "kick off" at the end of June', Sassoon later wrote in his *Memoirs of an Infantry Officer* (1930). Sassoon won a Military Cross later in the battle, but by the time he wrote his memoirs he had become viscerally opposed to the war. ('The safest thing to be said', Sassoon wrote of medal-winners, 'is that nobody knew how much a decoration was worth except the man who received it.'*)

Sassoon's memoirs are superb at recreating life in the trenches before and during the 'Big Push'. He recalled 'knocking my pipe out against one of the wooden props which held up the cramped little den, and staring irritably at my mud-encumbered boots, for I was always trying to keep squalor at bay, and the discomfort of feeling dirty and tickly all over was almost as bad as a bombardment.'[43] He suffered from 'trench mouth' (acute necrotizing ulcerative gingivitis), whose symptoms were

---

* He also said that the front-line infantry wanted to distinguish between their decorations and the General Staff's, and 'rightly insisted that medal ribbons earned at Base should be a different colour'.

painful bleeding gums, and wrote of how 'Trench life was an existence saturated by the external senses; and although our actions were domineered by military discipline, our animal instincts were always uppermost.' As for his men, 'I could never understand how they managed to keep as cheery as they did through such drudgery and discomfort, with nothing to look forward to but going over the top or being moved up to Flanders again.'[44] Although officers on leave were warned not to speak about it and there was no mention of it in the newspapers, even Sassoon's Aunt Evelyn, who lived in Kensington, London 'was aware of the impending onslaught... No one had any idea what the Big Push would be like, except that it would be much bigger than anything which had happened before.'[45] Sassoon and a friend, Captain Huxtable, 'decided, between us, that the Push would finish the war by Christmas'.

On the way up to the front just before the assault, Sassoon noted how as a staff officer was coming in the other direction, 'Larks were rejoicing aloft, and the usual symbolic scarlet poppies lolled over the sides of the communication trench; but he squeezed past us without so much as a nod, for the afternoon was too noisy to be idyllic, in spite of the larks and poppies which were so popular with war-correspondents.' Sassoon asked his brother officer, Julian Dadd, 'I suppose those brasshats do know a hell of a lot about it, don't they, Julian,' only to receive the reply that they had not done so at Loos, but 'They've got to learn their job as they go along, like the rest of us.'[46]

The Germans also knew perfectly well what was about to happen. The Württemberger 26th Reserve Division in the north of the sector had heard the din of supplies being delivered night after night, and their patrols had discovered saps—underground trenches dug directly towards enemy lines—within 90 yards (82 m) of their positions. The Germans also spotted preparations for the offensive through aerial reconnaissance as early as 7 April.[47] They also noticed that the RFC was flying more reconnoitering sorties than hitherto. German Intelligence had learnt from London newspapers—which exercised an only haphazard self-censorship—that a meeting of owners and workers at munition factories had been told by a cabinet minister on 2 June that the Whitsun bank holiday weekend of 9 to 12 June would be postponed until the end of July.[48] Crown Prince Rupprecht of Bavaria, commander of the 6th Army, regarded this as

WATCHING

*A German soldier perched facing a trench mirror
as he sits in a reconnoitering post.*

'the surest proof that there will be a great British offensive in a few weeks.'[49]

That same day, 2 June, Gen. Fritz von Below, commanding the German 2nd Army, asked for reinforcements to disrupt the Allied plans with a pre-emptive attack on the Ancre, although he did not get any because of the Brusilov Offensive in the east.[50] On 19 June Prince Rupprecht reported to his private diary that a large-scale attack on the 2nd Army was clearly imminent and on the 26th he named 1 July as the day he thought, from intelligence received by the German military attaché in Madrid, that the attack would take place. He started issuing uplifting Orders of the Day, saying that the English stood foremost in the way of peace and that a victory would speedily end the war.

The forty-seven-year-old commander of the German 6th Army on the Somme, Crown Prince Rupprecht of Bavaria was a wholly admirable character and perhaps the only royal commander of the entire war who fully deserved his command. A truly professional soldier who had interrupted his military career to study at the universities of Munich and Berlin, he was also widely travelled in the Middle and Far East. A serious student of military history, he proved a most competent battlefield commander. In the latter stages of the war he was an opponent of Ludendorff's 'scorched earth' policies and a proponent of peace in late 1917 once he could see the struggle was undoubtedly lost; during the Third Reich he became an avowed anti-Nazi, telling his cousin King George V in 1934 that Hitler (who loathed him) was insane. He went into exile in Florence once the Second World War had broken out. Prince Rupprecht had commanded the Bavarian I Army Corps since 1906, becoming a full general in 1913. On the outbreak of the First World War he was given command of the German 6th Army, with which he checked Gen. Noël de Castelnau's 2nd Army at the Battle of Lorraine in August 1914, although some in the army unfairly blamed him for not having achieved the much needed breakthrough on the Marne.[51] In giving Rupprecht command of the Northern Army Group forces on 28 August 1916, Ludendorff chose more than just a safe pair of hands, and on 17 December Rupprecht's Order of the Day stated: 'The greatest battle of the war, perhaps the greatest of all time, has been won.'[52] Rupprecht was promoted to field marshal soon after the first day of the Somme Offensive, yet by the time of the great Spring Offensive of 1918, he was thoroughly disillusioned about Germany's chances of victory. 'Ludendorff is a man of absolute determination,' he said of the architect of the gigantic Operation Michael, 'but determination alone is not enough, if it is not combined with clear-headed intelligence.'[53]

When the British attack came, the Germans were ready and waiting.

THREE

PREPARATIONS

—

'The artillery bombardment which preceded
the advance was in magnitude and terribleness beyond
the previous experience of Mankind.'[1]

CAPT. G. H. F. NICHOLS,
The 18th Division in the Great War

*

'Too many of the bravest and best perished,
seeking to compensate by valour for lack of experience
and the shortage of munitions, to the hazard
of the final victory and the detriment of
the future of the nation.'[2]

Preface to EDMONDS,
*History of the Great War: Military Operations
France and Belgium 1916*

CPL. SIDNEY APPLEYARD WAS BORN IN MAY 1894 IN Shoe Lane in the city of London, the son of a publisher and the second of three brothers. A quantity surveyor before volunteering on the outbreak of war aged twenty, he was initially rejected as unfit by the navy because his chest measurement was too small. In November 1915 the pressing need for volunteers meant that he managed to join the Territorial 9th London Regiment (Queen Victoria's Rifles), with which he commenced training in Hyde Park without a uniform and carrying a dummy rifle.[3] He certainly considered himself totally unqualified to fight when he and his battalion was shipped over to Flanders in May 1915.

'On the very long route marches we had to sing to keep our spirits up,' he recorded in his diary, 'and our platoon poet, Bill Bright, kept us going with some of his verse, such as:

> I'm a bomber, I'm a bomber
> Wearing a grenade,
> The Army's got me where it wants,
> I'm very much afraid.
> When decent jobs are going
> I never get a chance,
> Which shows what bloody fools we were
> To volunteer for France.[4]

As well as long route marches, Appleyard recalled how 'We had continuous practice throwing live bombs and had demonstrations of liquid fire which the Germans were now using. This was a very terrible and frightening affair but if one kept low in the trench it was quite harmless.'[5]

Sidney Appleyard's diary reminds us how ludicrously over-confident the High Command was when it came to the damage that the artillery would wreak on the German lines before the attack. 'We were informed by all officers from the Colonel downwards', he wrote,

> that after our tremendous artillery bombardment there would be very few Germans left to show fight, and they all fully expected us to carry the lines with very little resistance. Everybody was quite convinced by this time that this attack was really coming off, and was not going to fall through as similar affairs had in the past. So we all decided to make the most of our few days which remained and we thoroughly enjoyed ourselves. The distant rumble of artillery was distinctly heard during these days, and we heard very fine reports of the damage caused by our shells.[6] *

It was taken for granted throughout the General Staff that the artillery bombardment preliminary to the offensive would destroy the enemy's trenches, smash in his dugouts, cut through his barbed wire and prevent him replacing it, knock out machine gun emplacements and observation posts, and make life in the communication trenches, batteries, billets and support roads behind the lines completely intolerable. As Brig. Edmonds, the

* Appleyard was wounded in the Battle of the Somme and while recuperating he met a nurse called Rosie Phillips. He saw further service on the Western Front in 1917 before he was sent out to Aden. He was demobilized at the end of 1919, whereupon he qualified as a quantity surveyor, founded his own successful practice, and married Rosie. His is one of the very few happy endings in this book.

official historian of the battle for the Committee of Imperial Defence, was to put it:

> It was not expected that there would be effective gunfire or that his reserves would be able to come up... But in every attack thus far, the Germans had produced some surprise, and at the Somme it was to be deep mined dug-outs, with sometimes two storeys below ground,* sheltering machine guns and their crews from harm during the bombardment. The garrisons of the first position remained below ground, close packed, uncomfortable, short of food, depressed, but still alive and ready on their officers' orders, when the barrage lifted, to issue forth with morale unbroken; if there were neither parapets nor trenches, then to man with machine guns and rifles any shell-hole that came handy.[7]

This was what happened throughout the northern and central sector, with catastrophic results for the British assault.

In preparation for the 'Big Push', Gen. Sir Douglas Haig turned the entire Somme sector into a massive military encampment and supply dump. By 1 July 1916 the BEF numbered 660,000 effectives, increased from 450,000 at the start of the year.[8] Haig needed 400,000 men for the offensive as well as 100,000 horses, both as cavalry and to carry equipment. Horses were vital to the war effort for bringing up stores and supplies; 8 million served in the British army in the First World War, of which 1 million died. The offensive required an enormous logistical

---

* The German dugouts were sometimes up to 60 feet (18.2 m) underground. In Fricourt, 5 miles (8 km) from Albert, one was found with nine bedrooms with bunk beds, five exits, a bathroom and electricity for lights and bells.

operation, such as the laying of 7,000 miles (11,265 km) of signal cables buried 7 feet (2.1 m) deep, so that German shelling could not sever it. Road and rail transportation had to be built from scratch or improved and extended. (The troops resented the navvies who built the railway tracks but went nowhere near the front line and earned more than the infantryman's shilling—5p—a day.)

Fuel, food and water, arms and ammunition of all kinds—the British army fired an average of a million shells a week throughout the battle—medical supplies, postal services, trench and dugout construction, equine forage: these were just the bare basic requirements for maintaining an army in the field, let alone preparing it for easily the greatest offensive operation in the history of the British army.[9] In the final few weeks before the 'Big Push', airfields were prepared for the RFC, leave was cancelled, field gun ammunition was taken well forward and buried deep underground, the men were ordered to do constant bayonet practice, and graves were dug (though in the event nothing like enough). New helmets were issued, flat basins of khaki-painted manganese steel that were said to be capable of deflecting shrapnel, but which unlike the German helmets failed to protect the ears. Pigeons were issued to send messages back from captured trenches; imitation snipers' heads were set up to draw German fire; roads were screened with camouflage netting to hide them from enemy air reconnaissance.

'Dumps as big as small towns grew up almost overnight prepared to issue anything,' wrote John Harris in *Covenant with Death*, 'periscopes, grenades, compasses, rations, mortar bombs, smoke helmets, tools.'[10] These camouflage-covered dumps

A TRENCH MORTAR DUMP
Mortars were an ideal weapon in trench warfare: a high-trajectory weapon,
its bomb would drop down into trenches and wire emplacements.

seemed to expand all over the forward area. An order for Very
lights or Stokes bombs would bring men to a store packed with
rough wooden boxes full of lethal weaponry. Casualty clearing
stations and advanced field dressing stations were erected, and
gas cylinders weighing 180 lbs (81.5 kg) were carried forward
on poles by two men each, who had to wear gas masks in case
of leakages. Cart-loads of empty biscuit tins were meanwhile
driven up and down behind the lines to drown the noise of work
parties excavating mines, saps and jumping-off trenches. Huge
barbed wire compounds of several acres each were also con-
structed for the thousands of prisoners who were expected to
be captured. 'Great preparations have been made for the offensive,' Gunner Gwilym Ewart Davies of the Royal Artillery, who

only landed at Rouen on 13 June and had not yet been issued with a steel helmet, noted in his diary eight days later: 'Signs directing the way to different hospitals are nailed up in the trenches... Trolleys specially reserved for the wounded are to be found on the railway lines... Our airmen brought down two German observation balloons today. They set them ablaze by dropping bombs on them.'[11]

'It was evident to all that something out of the ordinary was impending, for men and guns continued to appear in ever growing quantities,' recalled 2nd-Lt. Geoffrey Fildes of the 2nd Battalion Coldstream Guards. 'Valleys that only a week before had been devoid of all occupants now began to assume an aspect of busy preparation. Huts and dugouts were being constantly erected, and the masses of materials assembled for the Royal Engineers became exceedingly great... Once again, as on the eve of Loos, we lived in an atmosphere of endless speculation.'[12] Fildes noted the new single-track railway built across the countryside to the north of the Coldstreams' position and how 'Every ravine and hollow behind the Fricourt ridge was being converted into a battery position, and trenching and mining operations were being pushed on at all possible speed throughout the neighbourhood.'[13] In his official report, Haig said that over one hundred pumping plants were installed for water and more than 120 miles (193 km) of water mains were laid.[14] Yet it has been estimated that even if Haig had broken through, the badly stretched BEF might not have been able to exploit the advantage due to sheer logistical difficulties.[15]

The visit the men dreaded more than any other was that from the Deputy Assistant Director of Medical Services (DADMS), whom Lt. Cecil Down of the 1/4th Gordon Highlanders described as 'the stormy petrel of the Western Front. Whenever he appears in the front system, there is trouble ahead. He comes into your dugout and says a few well-chosen words on the sanitation, or lack thereof, in your trenches, but all the time his eye is roving around your abode deciding how many stretcher cases could be accommodated in it.'[16] For the men in the trenches, the sight of the cerise band on the hat of the DADMS meant 'worse was in store' and the General Staff were expecting high casualties in their sector. Thereafter, Down recalled, one knew it was only a matter of time before you were called to the colonel's dugout along with all the other officers, where one would 'have a large document, labelled Secret and Confidential, in blue pencil, read out to you on the subject of your assaulting the German trenches, marked in red pencil, on the near date and at a time to be communicated later by special messenger.'[17]

At 5 a.m. on Friday, 24 June 1916, the Allied bombardment opened up along the whole 18 mile (29 km) front.[18] The rumble of artillery firing could be heard across the English Channel in Kent for the next month as the battle went on.[19] 'The din was terrific,' Capt. Herries of the 22nd Battalion Northumberland Fusiliers (Tyneside Scottish) wrote to his father in Newcastle just before the attack, 'so great in fact was the noise that although 20 feet [6 m] down in dugouts we were unable to sleep.'[20] The 4th Army deployed its 1,010 field guns and howitzers, 182 heavy guns and 245 heavy howitzers for this bombardment, and the French 40 guns and howitzers and 60 75 mm guns for gas shells.[21]

Designating 1 July as the first day of the Somme Offensive is slightly inaccurate, as the preliminary bombardment went on for a week beforehand. The infantry attack took place on the eighth day of the campaign from the point of view of the British artillery, and of course of the Germans on the receiving end. Since some 59 per cent of the casualties on the Western Front in the First World War were the result of artillery fire—soldiers rarely saw a live enemy from head to foot—it was vital that the bombardment should succeed.[22] For the moment it ended there would take place what has been called 'the race to the parapet', when the Germans who had survived the bombardment would try to get to the firing positions on their front-line trenches and the British would advance across no man's land. The Germans issuing out of their dugouts were of course much closer to their positions than the British coming forward under the protection of the barrage, who had to get past the barbed wire, all the while heavily encumbered by the absurd amounts of equipment they had to carry. On the first day of the Somme the Germans, who had survived the bombardment unscathed in their deep dugouts, got to the parapets long before the British, and had set up their machine guns in time for the appearance of the British infantry advancing towards them at walking pace.

At first, as memoranda between GHQ and the 4th Army tell us, it had been suggested that a forty-eight-hour preliminary bombardment would be enough, but the 4th Army argued that this would not succeed in cutting the barbed wire, so the shelling was extended to five days. The bombardment was divided into two general phases, the first two days entirely devoted to field artillery cutting the wire in no man's land while the heavy guns registered other targets. The next three days were for the bombarding of German trenches and fortified villages, with further shelling directed at points where the Germans had repaired the wire. The 2-in. mortars were relied upon to deal with the first lines of German wire, with 18 lb guns firing deeper, and the second-line German positions—4,000 yards (3,658 m) from the British lines—were pulverized by medium artillery. However, this meant that the medium guns, of which there were far too few, had too much to do, including counter-battery fire at German guns, attacking anything that moved on roads, and additional wire-cutting duties. Destroying the wire in front of the second line of German defences, the hardest of the tasks, was given the lowest priority, though in the event this would matter very little as so few British troops ever got that far.

In the southern sector the French artillery barrage was far more concentrated and saturated the German front line, preventing the Germans from winning the race to the parapets. The French 75 mm gun could fire 15 shells a minute, and despite there being more than twice the number of British infantry as French, the French put down twice the weight of bombardment.[23] Because tactical surprise was achieved in the French sector and by XIII Corps, which was also where the counter-battery fire had been the strongest, it was the most successful part of the battlefield from the Allied perspective. The French attack took place between Maricourt and Curlu south of the Somme at 9.30 a.m., allowing their artillery to support the British for the first two hours of the attack. Indeed, the only place where the German deep dugouts were penetrated by shellfire

FRENCH 75MM FIELD GUN
*This field gun with the highest rate of fire of its generation enabled the
French to put down twice the weight of bombardment as the British.*

was on the Montauban front, where the artillery batteries were largely French.[24] The three French corps had nearly one hundred more heavy guns than the five British corps.[25] French shells also worked far better than those of their British counterparts, because they had more sensitive fuses that exploded on immediate impact with the ground rather than when they were buried into it.

In fact, very worryingly, a large number of British shells—three-quarters of which were made in America—simply did not go off.[26] According to German observers, 60 per cent of British medium-calibre shells and nearly every shrapnel shell failed to explode, although British sources suggest it was closer to one-third.[27] Such was the desperate need for artillery ammunition that normal quality controls were ignored by the War Office, to disastrous effect. When ground was captured, it was often found to be pitted with unexploded British shells as large as 9.2 in. calibre. Other shells went off prematurely, killing British artillerymen and destroying guns. Historians still debate why there were quite so many dud shells. Shortages of skilled labour, lack of advanced machinery and a lack of precision in the manufacturing of shells and fuses on behalf of the mass of sub-contractors that the Ordnance Department, Ministry of Munitions and War Office were forced to rely upon after the breakdown in supply in the spring of 1915 probably explain most of it.[28] Britain was strong in heavy industry, but had tended to lag behind Germany in precision machine-tooling and the light engineering of products needed to produce working shells. Live, unexploded shells would turn up on the battlefield regularly for the next century.[29] (I saw some freshly discovered ones by the roadside near Serre in 2014.)

Maj. Ynyr[*] Probert of the Royal Artillery won a Military Cross at the storming of the Hindenburg Line in 1918 after recovering from severe wounds received on the Somme in the autumn of 1916, but he lived to be one hundred years old and become the oldest Old Etonian.[†] His father, who also fought in the First World War, was Queen Victoria's daughter Princess Louise's comptroller and his mother was Mary Badcock, the little girl whose photograph Lewis Carroll and John Tenniel took as their

---

[*] The unusual name derived from his ancestor Ynyr, King of Gwent.
[†] In the 1970s when his radiologist gloomily announced, 'Your X-Rays show your back to be full of metal', Probert replied, 'You don't want to touch that stuff, it's been there for sixty years.'

inspiration for the original illustrations of *Alice in Wonderland*. Probert left school aged seventeen and spent six months at the Royal Arsenal at Woolwich ('The Shop') before being commissioned to go to France in October 1915. He took part in the 1 July 1916 offensive as an artillery forward observation officer, and kept a diary which became covered in mud and blood but is still readable.

In January 1916 he noted: 'Ammunition was very short and although we were already getting some supplies from America it was of very dubious quality resulting in many [British] casualties from "prematures". There were also many duds.'[30] (Only five weeks before, on 26 May, he had recorded: 'One of the hazards of returning from the Observation Post in the evenings walking across the open was the crowd of heavy, noisy Maybugs which lived in the oakwoods.* They struck with considerable force, necessitating carrying something like your tin hat in front of your face.'[31]

Probert noted how only heavy shells were capable of destroying the German deep dugouts, but although the British fired 188,500 of them they were not effective in the centre and north of the battlefield. Moreover, two-thirds of the shells were fired at the barbed wire rather than the enemy trenches. The British could devote only 180 guns to fire at enemy batteries, and this was not enough to suppress the German artillery, which could cut off those British troops who did manage to make it into the German trenches by making no man's land impassable for reinforcement and resupply.[32]

---

* The maybugs are still there today.

The responsibility for counter-battery fire as well as the destruction of German trenches, dugouts and strongpoints was kept at corps level in the British army, unlike the French, who devolved such decision-making to the divisions. After the first day, Major-Gen. de Lisle recommended that heavy howitzers at least should be placed under divisional control so that 'all the local knowledge of the Divisional artillery would be utilized in the important work of the destruction of the enemy's main trench line'.[33] Of course this could only have been achieved with far more limited objectives than the three defensive lines that Haig wanted to attack. Because reports from minus 30 hours right down to near Zero Hour were telling divisional commanders that the entrances to the German dugouts had not been blocked by the bombardment, the British guns should all have been directed onto the front-line trenches rather than further back. The French 6th Army in the southern sector devolved artillery to the divisional level with great success, devastating the German front-line trenches with trench mortar and howitzer fire. The French also enthusiastically engaged in the all-important counter-battery fire that the British corps to the north neglected. French 75s poured shells and often gas into the German artillery positions on the southern sector and in front of XIII Corps at Montauban.

The sheer multiplicity of targets required to put into effect Haig's ambitious plans meant that the German front-line trenches were battered but survived. 'I consider that one of the chief factors that contributed to the failure of our infantry in [the 86th Brigade at Auchonvillers] sector to penetrate the line anywhere', wrote Lt.-Col. Douglas Evans Forman of

147th Brigade Royal Field Artillery after the war, 'was the fact that the enemy front trench had not been sufficiently crumpled up by our heavy artillery beforehand, with the result that the Germans were able to circulate freely in it once our attack was launched.'[34] This estimation echoes the contemporary views of the official war diarists of the 87th and 88th Brigades. In the last ten days of June, the German 2nd Army only lost 2,478 killed and missing and 4,482 wounded from the bombardment, two-thirds of them the result of French bombardment in the south.[35]

The limiting factor with field guns since the Napoleonic War had always been the hauling strength of six horses, which was around 4,000 lbs (1,814 kg). This included the carriage and limber as well as the metal of the gun itself. Improved materials and techniques had halved the weight of cannon, allowing armour-plated shields and recoil mechanisms to be added, so that a century after the Napoleonic Wars, an 800 lb nickel steel gun could fire the same 12 or 15 lb projectile as a Napoleonic gun of twice the weight. It also had significantly greater muzzle velocity, a flatter trajectory, longer range and a more powerful propellant charge. The 75 mm shell, for example, contained 1.76 lb of high explosive (HE) compared to about half a pound of black powder in pre-1893 shells.[36] A gun of the American Civil War could fire shrapnel 2,000 yards (1,828 m), or shell nearly 4,000 (3,657 m) at a speed of 1,090 ft (c. 332 m) per second, whereas an artillery piece in 1914 was capable of firing 6,500 yards (5,943 m) with shrapnel, or 8,500 yards (7,772 m) with shell at 1,770 ft (c. 540 m) per second.[37] The sheer expenditure of shells massively increased also: at the Battle of Gettysburg in 1863 the Union army fired 32,780, at Sha Ho in 1904 the Russians fired 274,360, at Neuve Chapelle in 1915 the British fired 197,000, but at the Somme the Allies fired 1,627,824 during the seven days preceding the assault. Yet, as the official historian noted, even this 'did not accomplish what had been confidently predicted'.[38]

Two-thirds of the Allied shellfire was of shrapnel rather than HE.[39] The army's nickname for HE shells was 'whizzbangs'.* 'I learned to disregard whatever noise didn't immediately concern me', states the hero of *Covenant with Death*. 'The howitzer shells that sounded like express trains rushing through the air didn't concern us at all—they were heading for the rear areas—but I kept my eyes and ears well open for the local stuff—the whizzbangs which exploded again and again like a lumping cracker, and the grotesquely somersaulting *minenwerfer* bombs.'[40] The men could not cook their own meals in case they attracted attention from the *minenwerfer*.

Of the heavy guns and howitzers used by the British, many were obsolete or of extemporized patterns. The British artillery could not prevail in counter-battery fire for the simple reason that the German heavy batteries were out of range of the British 60-pounders and 6 in. howitzers and the older 4.7 in guns. Only a few super-heavy guns could reach the German heavy batteries, which were therefore capable of operating in relative safety throughout the battle, except in the French sector.[41]

Barbed wire was originally invented as a means of enclosing livestock in the American West, but its military application in holding up infantry attacks was soon appreciated. German barbed

---

* The Germans also had nicknames for different types of ordnance; mortar bombs of a particular type were called 'toffee apples', for example.

6-INCH HOWITZER
A mainstay of the Royal Garrison Artillery,
there were 104 of them in action on 1 July.

wire on the Somme could be 6 feet (1.8 m) high—often twice as high as Allied barbed wire—and was laid twice as thickly, anywhere between 4.5 yards (4.1 m) and 9 yards (8.2 m) wide.[42] The barbed wire in front of the trenches on the Somme was strung fairly loosely from screw pickets or iron posts, or more rarely wooden posts, which were much more vulnerable. German barbed wire had to be 30 yards (27.4 m) from their trenches, otherwise the British could throw Mills bombs from behind it.[43] There were often narrow lanes in the wire through which patrols and raiding parties could pass. The Germans stored wire in forward trenches, to be pushed out into no man's land even when under fire.[44] Clearing barbed wire in preparation for an attack was notoriously hard. The infantry used wire-cutters, though this had to be done at night. The Royal Engineer sappers could also plant small demolition charges to clear the wire on such nocturnal raids. Bangalore torpedoes blasted gaps in the wire. But all these expedients were necessarily small scale and highly risky; the bulk of the work was left to the artillery. A useful tool in 1916 was the 3 in. trench mortar which had a fuse to burst the shell on impact, so a 50 lb bomb could cut a large circle of wire.[45] (Firing at barbed wire with HE has been likened to shooting at a fishing net with a shotgun.)[46]

Shrapnel was the best available method for destroying barbed wire in 1916, even though it lost effectiveness at long range and was not much use against German second-line wire defences. It also required skill in firing and observing, and the Territorial and Kitchener volunteer gunners were still learning on the job. Wire could not be seen on the reverse slopes, and was hard to spot from long distances. Sometimes long grass grew up around it, further hampering observation. Yet Lt.-Gen. Hunter-Weston of VIII Corps reported before 1 July that the enemy wire was so badly damaged that 'the troops could walk in', even though other more junior officers 'could see it standing strong and well'.[47]

By 1917 there was a new fuse and HE could be fired by howitzers onto reverse slopes, but all that was too late for the men of the Somme, or at least those who survived the first day. For 1 July, each field battery was assigned a sector to try to cut gaps in the wire, the guns in the centre firing straight and the outer ones aiming inwards. The planners expected there would be easily enough gaps for the attackers to get through to make the offensive a success.[48]

While on leave, Siegfried Sassoon bought two pairs of rubber-handled wire-cutters from the Army & Navy Stores in London, as his company did not have enough of them and what they did have were of 'savage bluntness'. He used them the night before the assault to cut some of the wire ahead of the Manchester Regiment, as he was concerned about what the Manchesters would say about his regiment the Royal Welch Fusiliers if the wire was not properly cut.[49] When he went out that night with a party of eight, he found 'More than once we were driven in by shells which landed in front of our trench (some of them were our own dropping short)', and it took him three and a half hours, 'but the hedge hadn't suffered much damage, it seemed'. With the fear of machine-gunners and snipers, Sassoon wrote, 'It was rather like going out to weed a neglected garden after being told there might be a tiger among the gooseberry bushes.'[50] Small wonder he was later put up for the Victoria Cross.

Chlorine gas had first been used on the battlefield at Langemarck, Ypres, on 22 April 1915. By 1 July 1916 the protection issued to the troops consisted of a 'small box respirator' with a filter cartridge carried in a haversack on the wearer's chest, connected to the respirator by tube. Warnings of the use of gas came from klaxons, bells, banging on an empty shell case or even football rattles. After problems with gas at Loos, the British did not envelop the German trenches in gas prior to 1 July, although, as one historian attests, 'nothing else could have neutralized dugouts burrowed into the Picardy chalk to depths of forty feet.'[51]

Gas was released day and night later on in the battle, at irregular intervals to increase the terror, but was not used strategically on the first day of the offensive, as it ought to have been.

The Somme was not the most heavily bombarded battlefield of the First World War. Verdun suffered more in terms of shells per square metre. Nor was the preliminary bombardment the longest of the war—those at the battles of the Aisne, Chemin des Dames and the Ypres salient were longer. Yet for all that, 1.6 million shells were fired and those Germans who had to stay above ground during the preliminary bombardment for any reason, were, in the words of Philip Gibbs, 'blown to fragments of flesh'.[52] The vast majority went into the dugouts for protection. In the BBC television series *The Great War* broadcast for the war's half-centenary in 1964, John Terraine's script stated that under the great British bombardment 'even the rats became hysterical'.[53] Perhaps they did, but the Germans generally were not, and waited patiently for days for it to end and the race to the parapet to start. One German in a dugout on 30 June wrote of how, 'We are quite shut off from the rest of the world. Nothing comes to us, no letters. The English keep such a barrage on our approaches it is terrible. Tomorrow evening it will be seven days since this bombardment began. We cannot hold out much longer. Everything is shot to pieces.'[54] A German prisoner told Gibbs: 'Those who went outside were killed or wounded. Some of them had their heads blown off, and some of them had both their legs torn off, and some of them their arms. But we went on taking turns in the hole, although those who went outside knew that it was their time to die, most likely. At last most of those who came into the hole were wounded, some of them badly, so that we lay in blood.'[55]

'In particular, one concentration of fire at a quarter past two outdid anything there had been up to that point', another German soldier, the writer Ernst Jünger (see page 142), recalled. 'A hail of heavy shells struck all around my dugout. We stood fully armed on the shelter steps, while the light of our little candle stumps reflected glitteringly off the wet, mildewed walls. Blue smoke streamed in through the entrances, and earth crumbled off the ceiling.'[56] The atmosphere in the German dugouts, and especially the bad air, was recalled by Kresten Andresen, a Danish-speaking schoolteacher from Holstein who spent eight hours on 30 June digging and repairing connecting trenches 12 miles (19.3 km) behind the front lines. 'When you've been lying there asleep for five or six hours you get a tight, spongy feeling across your chest as if you had asthma, but it goes away fairly quickly once you get into the fresh air and light.'[57] The mattresses were stuffed with wood shavings that clumped together in lumps and the beds were so narrow the men had to sleep on their sides, with their hips under one of the few slats.*

There was fine weather till 23 June, when it broke and a thunderstorm brought torrential rain, which continued to fall intermittently for the next week, with the skies never less than overcast. Because the weather was so bad just before the attack, the RFC could not get their planes up to look for the German guns, and its work was seriously interrupted for the rest of the month. It also meant that there was a good deal of water in the

---

* Andresen, who did not even like Germans, later died on the Somme, though his body was never found.

bottom of the trenches, which seeped through puttees and turned the soil into clinging mud that stuck to the men's boots in stiff blocks, and made each step feel as if the wearer were lifting weights.

'The whole heaven is lighted up by the glare of the gun flashes,' recalled Pte. Frank Williams of the 88th Field Ambulance of the Royal Army Medical Corps (RAMC) on 25 June. 'The night sky was a mass of lurid light from the star shells and the incessant flash of guns, while the scream of aerial torpedoes and tear gas shells and the general booming artillery was punctuated by the explosion of mighty monsters of destruction, the whole combined coming to us with an ominous rumble, like the sea on a cavernous coast.'[58] Yet a captured letter from a German called Otto Sauer, 'written under heavy shellfire' to his girlfriend Sophie, read 'Dear Sophie, Your loving postcard I received with joy, many best thanks. I am otherwise in good order, am still thank God healthy and jolly.'[59] It was a bad sign when even under this bombardment Germans stayed 'healthy and jolly', even if he was exaggerating.

The next day, 26 June, after Lt. William Bloor's C Battery of 146th Brigade of the Royal Field Artillery had fired 598 shells continually from dawn to 1.30pm, Bloor noted how on the enemy's side:

> The whole countryside was just one mass of flame, smoke and earth thrown up sky high. About 5,000 shells per diem are pitching on a front of about 500 yards [457 m]. Whilst observing, I could not resist feeling sorry for the wretched atoms of humanity crouching behind their ruined parapets, and going through hell itself. Modern

war is the most cruel thing I ever heard of, and the awful
ordeal of those poor devils, even though they are Boche,
must be impossible to describe.[60]

Interestingly, Pte. Frank Williams also noted how at a service the
day before, 'the crashing roar of some of the [artillery] reports
made me pray for the Germans', although of course he would
have been praying for their souls rather than their survival.

That same day, 26 June, Capt. Harold Bidder of the 1st South
Staffordshire Regiment, recalled the sights and sounds of the
bombardment:

> There were heavy clouds, and under them a red band of
> sunset in the north-east. The continuous flashes of the
> guns played on the clouds like summer lightning, while
> over the German trenches the shrapnel was bursting in
> white flares, the High Explosive in dull red glows… Our
> shells whistled overhead, and, as it got darker still, showed
> as red shooting stars whizzing across. We opened up with
> two machine guns. The noise of a stream of machine-gun
> bullets is like waves on a stormy beach, a prolonged swish.
> The biggest noise was the earthquake crashing of the
> French trench mortars.[61]

Cpl. Appleyard remembered marching up to the front on 27
June, singing 'Blighty Land' and 'I Want to Go Home'. 'Great
scenes were to be seen along the roads and long streams of
ammunition columns and motor lorries were making their ways
to the scene of operations', he wrote in his diary. 'The guns were
now heard distinctly and the crump of our big guns encouraged
us greatly for we infantrymen always like to know that we have
got good artillery behind us.'[62]

Gunner F. J. G. Gambling was an unmarried Worcestershire artillery signaller telephonist with B Battery, Royal Field Artillery in the 97th Brigade of 21st Division. On 27 June he noted in his diary: 'At 7.30 a.m. on the morning of the fourth day [of the bombardment] a batch of prisoners were taken by us. A more dejected crew could not be found in a week's march. Dirty, unshaven with hang-dog expressions on their faces.'[63]

Of course the Germans responded with their own artillery bombardments. Working in the outside behind the lines all morning, trying to build a splinter-proof shelter for their observation post on 28 June, Lt. William Bloor and his party were bombarded either by German shells or by a British shell that

THE APPLEYARD
BROTHERS
Corporal Sidney
Appleyard, left, was
initially rejected as unfit
when he first volun-
teered but eventually
joined Queen Victoria's
Rifles. He was wounded
on the Somme and lived
to see the war's end.

went off too early. Just as they were finishing the job at around noon, Bdr. Greenwood was hit and Bloor recalled how,

> It was a horrible wound in the stomach, and all the
> bleeding was inward. In ten seconds this fine big fellow,
> who was as strong as a lion and always had a beautiful
> ruddy colour, was writhing on the ground and his face
> was green in hue and he was in awful agony. I knew there
> was no hope for him from the first, but told him the usual
> lies about it being nothing serious, etc. I got an old wire
> bed out of a deserted billet near and we carried him to the
> dressing station half a mile [800 m] away.[64]

Greenwood died later that afternoon. Revd Montague Acland 'Monty' Bere was Anglican chaplain to the 43rd Casualty Clearing Station, part of the 3rd Army. After Marlborough, Oxford, and sixteen years as a vicar among the slums of West Ham and Leytonstone in London's East End, he volunteered to be a field chaplain aged fifty. 'One has had the chance of shooting a beam of light in the darkness' was how he summed up his service, during which time he contracted diphtheria.[65] On 28 June 1916 he wrote to his wife back in Bovington, Dorset: 'The shell-shock men are sad. One is an officer who has forgotten his home address, another is dumb and so on.'[66] The next day he added:

> There is nothing much to be done with dying people in
> this sort of place—they come in and stay unconscious.
> The wounded are practically all Londoners so far and are
> wonderfully entertaining even if they are short of an arm
> or a leg.* A convoy of wounded on arrival is an extraor-

---

* One cockney, who had just had his left arm amputated, described the latest type of British bomb, ending, 'If that doesn't put the wind up Fritz, nothing will.'

dinary sight, particularly the walking cases. They beggar description—rags, dirt and bandages, trousers torn off at the knee, unwashed and without any expression… The men come in apparently stark naked from time to time. One was sent to the train with nothing on but identity disc and small bandage.[67]

Siegfried Sassoon recalled Wednesday 28 June as 'miserably wet. Junior officers, being at a loss to know where to put them-selves, were continually meeting one another along the muddy street, and gathering in groups to exchange cheerful remarks; there was little else to be done, and solitude produced the sink-ing feeling appropriate to the circumstances.'[68] That same day the Lonsdale Battalion, part of 97th Brigade of 32nd Division, paraded in fighting order to go over the top, but on the 29th word came postponing the attack until further notice. The British pre-liminary bombardment was supposed to have ended with the Z Day attack on 29 June but it was extended forty-eight hours after the very wet weather on the 26th, 27th and 28th. The Lonsdales then heard nothing till the night of 30 June when they were told they would be going over the top at 7 a.m. the next morning.*[69]

'A little rain made a big difference to life up there,' Sieg-fried Sassoon recorded, 'and the weather had been wet enough to make the duckboards wobble.'[70] He added: 'In spite of the anti-climax (which made us feel that perhaps this was only going to be a second edition of the Battle of Loos), my personal impression was that we were setting out for the other end of nowhere.'[71] 'In the evening', Gunner Gambling recorded in his

* In the event it was 7.30 a.m.

diary on 29 June, 'Fritz opened fire with some of his gas shells, dropping them dangerous near a battery in our rear, and of course, the wind blowing in our direction, we got a good amount of the gas, but he finished up having done no damage at all (as per usual.)'[72] There is a terrible irony to this last comment, as Gambling was himself to die from the effects of gas poisoning a few years after the war.

Cpl. Appleyard also remembered 29 June: 'The Thursday was spent in bayonet fighting and bomb throwing [practice], and in the afternoon we had an enjoyable game of cricket, which helped to take the weight of coming events off our minds... According to a report from the 8th Middlesex, our guns were effectively smashing up the Huns' positions. A patrol who successfully entered the trenches reported that the first two lines of German trenches had already been evacuated.'[73] Like so many rumours swirling around at that time, it was wildly over-optimistic. 'Everybody seemed anxious to dispose of their remaining cash,' Appleyard wrote of 30 June, 'so we bought champagne, which put us all in good spirits and everybody was merry and bright when time for parade was called.'[74] That night just outside Souastre, 'an excellent view of the artillery duel was witnessed, and the flashes from the guns and the bursting of the shells formed a grand spectacle, and it was very fine to watch this from a distance but totally different when we entered the inferno.'[75]

In the days just before the assault, Sassoon also noticed how:

> There was harmony in our Company Mess, as if our
> certainty of a volcanic future had put an end to the

occasional squabblings which occurred when we were on each other's nerves. A rank animal healthiness pervaded our existence during those days of busy living and inward foreboding. The behaviour of our servants expressed it; they were competing for the favours of a handsome young woman in the farmhouse, and a comedy of primitive courtship was being enacted in the kitchen. Death would be lying in wait for the troops next week, and now the flavour of life was doubly strong.[76]

As the regimental servants wooed the pretty farm girl, their officers played tug-of-war against the officers of the 9th Battalion.

Going up to the front on 30 June, Capt. Harold Bidder of the 1st South Staffordshires noted, 'By way of a cheerful send-off, a gramophone in one of the houses I passed was playing the 'Dead March' in *Saul!*'[77] That same day Pte. Frank Hawkings of the 1st/9th London Regiment (Queen Victoria's Rifles) noted: 'Today is my birthday, and anyone will concede that it is hardly an appropriate time to have one. We suddenly got order to move this afternoon.' He was eighteen. 'Am feeling dreadfully tired,' he wrote at 1 a.m. once he reached the front-line fire trench, 'so I'm going to try to snatch a little sleep, though I don't expect to be very successful.' Gunner Gambling noted in his diary that day, 'At 6 p.m. a chum and myself were taking a stroll after coming off duty in what was a nice small village just behind our positions and there we realized what war really was, as we watched ambulance after ambulance go slowly by, filled with the wounded.'[78] And that was the night *before* the big attack.

Although they were ordered to get some sleep on the night of 30 June, many of the troops, such as LCpl. Arthur Cook of

the 1st Somerset Light Infantry, knew that '[we could rest] our weary limbs, but sleep was out of the question'.[79] Sassoon later recalled 'the blood-red sky' of that night and how 'we halted with the sunset behind us and the whole sky mountainous with the magnificence of retreating rainclouds'. He thought 'the symbolism of the sunset was wasted on the rank and file, who were concerned with the not infrequent badness of their boots, the discomfort caused by perspiration, and the toils and troubles of keeping pace with what was required of them.'[80] The next day another poet, Cecil Day-Lewis of the RFC, recorded the situation from the air at 7 a.m., during the crescendo of the preliminary bombardment: 'Half an hour to go! The whole salient, from Beaumont Hamel down to the marshes of the Somme, covered to a depth of a hundred yards with the coverlet of white wool—smoking shell bursts! It was the greatest bombardment in the history of the war, the greatest in the history of the world... Nothing could live under that rain of splintering steel.'[81]

He was wrong.

BRITISH TROOPS WAIT PENSIVELY
Above: *British troops rest on their way to the trenches,*
with wire cutters attached to their rifles;
below: *Waiting for the order to advance on Beaumont Hamel*
on the first day of the Battle of the Somme.

FOUR

ZERO HOUR

I, that on my familiar hill / Saw with uncomprehending eyes /
A hundred of thy sunsets spill / Their fresh and
sanguine sacrifice, / Ere the sun swings his noonday sword /
Must say good-bye to all of this— / By all delights
that I shall miss, / Help me to die, O Lord.[1]

LT. NOEL HODGSON MC,
9th Devonshire Regiment

*

'Nobody could put on paper the whole truth of what
went on here on Saturday and during Saturday night—
and no one could read it, if he did, without being sick.'[2]

REVD MONTAGUE BERE,
*chaplain to the 43rd Casualty Clearing
Station, to his wife, 4 July 1916*

'ON JULY 1ST THE WEATHER, AFTER AN EARLY MIST was of the kind commonly called heavenly', recalled Siegfried Sassoon. He and his brother officers breakfasted at 6 a.m., 'unwashed and apprehensive', an empty ammunition box for their table. At 6.45 the final bombardment began, and there was nothing to do but sit round our candle until the tornado ended. For more than forty minutes the air vibrated and the earth rocked and shuddered. Through the sustained uproar the tap and rattle of machine guns could be identified; but except for the whistle of bullets no retaliation came our way until a few 5.9 [in.] shells shook the roof of our dugout.' He and another officer 'sat speechless, deafened and stupefied by the seismic state of affairs, and when he lit a cigarette the match flame staggered crazily'.[3]

Cpl. Appleyard of the Queen Victoria's Rifles noted how 'Every gun in the sector fired rapid. This was kept up for an hour, at the end of which we sent over our smoke bombs. I witnessed the spectacle from the old original front line and it was the finest spectacle I have ever seen. The smoke varied in colour and as each cloud intermingled with the other, it formed beautiful tints.'[4]

'The sun rose higher,' wrote another observer of that morning, 'and birds chirped and fed in the charlock that garnished some of the trenches.'[5] Another recalled: 'It seemed years before the first ray of light appeared in the Heavens, but gradually the light grew stronger showing up the long line of khaki-clad boys.'[6] But for all its poetic delightfulness, the sun was in fact to pose a major problem for the soldiers as they prepared to clamber out of their trenches to do battle. Some British commanders wanted to attack at dawn, before the German machine-gunners could set their ranges properly. The Tommies (as the Germans nicknamed them)—who were generally attacking eastwards except in the southern sector—would otherwise have the rising sun in their eyes. Gen. Rawlinson pressed the French to accept an attack before sunrise, but, as Brig. Edmonds recorded in the *Official History*: 'The splendid chance of surprise offered by an assault in the early morning before the enemy machine-gunners could see very far was lost because the proposal for an early start was definitely rejected by the French, who even wished to make Zero Hour 9 a.m. instead of 7.30 a.m.'[7] This was a repetition of what had happened at Loos, where Gen. Foch had ordered French infantry not to attack until a full four hours after artillery observation was possible. Yet near the Somme River the mist was heavy, and although it cleared on the uplands it was still too thick at 7.30 a.m. for the German trenches to be seen clearly from the artillery observation posts before the attack.[8]

The men were massed in the assembly trenches by 4 a.m., so there was time to write last letters home. 'There is a big attack coming off very shortly, and we are in it', Lt. Malcolm White—a Shrewsbury schoolmaster in his mid-twenties who had enlisted in April 1915 and was with the 1st Rifle Brigade in the 4th Division north of Beaumont Hamel—wrote to his family.

> And there is just a minute to scribble a line to you with my love and greeting. We all hope it will be a success, though it will be a difficult business, I am sure. Our job will be to

take the front system of trenches in this area. Man, I can't
write a letter. There is much to think, but nothing to say
really. I dare say this will not reach you, but I have asked
a friend to send it for me when censorship does not apply
any longer... And now, I just want to say to you all, that,
if I don't come through it, you must all be quite cheerful
about it. I am quite happy about it, though of course I
can't deny that I'm quite keen to come home again... It
seems to me that, if I die in this action, it gives me a great,
simple chance to make up for a lot of selfishness in the
past... That's my view of it. It's not priggish—I hope it
doesn't sound like that. It is also a great comfort to think
of you all going on, living the same happy lives that we
have led together, and of the new generation coming into
it all. I can't write more, My dearest love to you all.[9]

Leading his men in the 1st Rifle Brigade's attack on Beaumont
Hamel, White was hit but not badly wounded, until a shell
landed nearby soon afterwards and killed him.[*]

Morale was high among the men waiting to attack that morning, especially once the bombardment intensified at 7.20 a.m.[10]
They understood that they would have to fight, but expected
that they would be matched against an enemy incapacitated and
demoralized by the week-long artillery barrage. Perhaps typical was the experience of Edward 'Ted' Higson who had volunteered on the outbreak of war for the Clerks and Warehousemen
Battalion of the Manchester Pals (18th Battalion Manchester
Regiment). They had been sent to France in November 1915 and
when they reached the front the next month 'As we approached

---

[*] His corpse was never identified; his name is engraved on the Thiepval Memorial to the Missing.

THE FINAL MOMENTS
The Lancashire Fusiliers fixing their bayonets
prior to the assault on Beaumont Hamel.

the firing line, we heard first of all the guns booming and many of us wondered how we should behave under fire, hoping for a steady nerve and a brave heart.'[11] By 30 June 1916, 'Everybody was eager to be "over the top",* our first big stunt… There were no white faces, no trembling limbs. In their hearts they were hoping to come through safely, not for their own sake but for the sake of those at home, but on the other hand they were quite prepared to die for the glorious cause of freedom and love.'[12]†
As for the sound of the bombardment's great finale: 'Hundreds

---

* Another phrase for it was 'to hop the bags', as in hop over the sandbags that lined the top of the trenches.
† It is quite clear from the rest of Higson's memoir – which he based on his war diary – that there was no irony intended here.

of guns were firing as quickly as they could be loaded; the noise was so intense that one could not hear what the man next to you was saying... to this day I wonder why the drums of our ears were not burst open.'[13]

The 'race to the parapet' is something of a misnomer, because one side—the British—all too often did not treat it as a race at all. That is evident from the vast amount of equipment each man was expected to carry. After climbing the ladders and going over the top of the trench, they walked forward with their .303-in. Lee-Enfield SMLE Mark 2 1907 rifles[*] carried across their chests in front of them at a slope, each with its 18-in. steel bayonet fixed to the barrel. Yet as well as those vital weapons, the men were loaded down terribly. The 29th Division, for example, ordered that:

> Each infantryman will carry rifle and equipment, 170 rounds of small arms ammunition, one iron ration and the rations for the day of the assault, two sandbags in belt, two [pineapple-shaped No. 36] Mills Bombs, steel helmet,[†] smoke [i.e. gas] helmet in satchel, water bottle and haversack[‡] on back, also first [aid] field dressing and identity disc. A waterproof sheet should also be taken.

[*] The sloped bolt action of the Lee-Enfield gave it a superior firing rate to the French and German rifles.
[†] For some reason called a 'tin hat'. Most of the men wore their chin-strap behind since it had been noticed that steel helmets struck by flying pieces of shell had a habit of spinning sharply upwards, giving a violent jerk to the chin confined in a chin-strap.
[‡] Which was required to include shaving gear and a spare pair of socks. The men had to be clean-shaven (except for officers, who tended to wear moustaches) so the gas masks fitted.

Troops of the second and third waves will carry only 120
rounds of ammunition. At least 40 per cent of the infantry
will carry shovels, and 10 per cent will carry picks.[14]

Many men carried their shovels across their chests for extra protection. As though this personal kit were not heavy enough, a
huge amount of other military equipment also had to be carried
into no man's land. The 88th Brigade (which included the Newfoundlanders), for example, had to share out between the four
battalions a total of 1,600 flares, 64 bundles of 5-foot wooden
pickets, 16 sledge-hammers, 640 wire-cutters and pairs of hedg-
ing gloves, 512 special haversacks for carrying Lewis machine
gun magazines, 32 trench bridges, 33 Bangalore torpedo tubes,
and some 7-foot trench ladders. Some units also carried pigeon
baskets, signalling gear, drums of telephone wire and tins of
grey paint to put the unit's identification on every artillery piece
captured. Those carrying barbed wire carried 90 lbs (41 kg) of
it. Small wonder that the leather straps that held the kit bit into
the men's shoulders, as the average infantryman was required
to carry half his own bodyweight across no man's land, under
fire.[15] 'The total weight carried per man was about 66 lbs [30
kg],' recorded the *Official History*, 'which made it difficult to get
out of a trench, impossible to move quicker than a slow walk, or
to rise and lay down quickly.'[16] As a footnote, Brig. Edmonds
pointed out that: 'This overloading of the men is by many infantry officers regarded as one of the principal reasons of the heavy
losses and failure of their battalions, for their men could not
get through the machine gun zone with sufficient speed.'[17] The
men also wore a woollen 'khaki drill' tunic which got very hot on

that sweltering July day, puttees, hobnail boots and trousers so uncomfortable that the Ulster Division cut them into shorts.[18]

Just before the attack, the men were given a hot meal (often stews), hot sweet tea and a tot of rum.* The food was carried up at night in large containers and was no longer particularly hot, but there were few complaints as it was often better than the food they ate back in Britain.† The daily rum ration came in large jars with SRD stamped on them, meaning 'Special Ration Distribution', which the Tommies joked stood for 'Seldom Reaches Destination'. The coffee that Bert Payne of the 1st City (Manchester Pals) Battalion 18th Manchesters drank just before going into battle had been brewed in empty fuel cans that the quartermaster, who had run out of jugs and urns, had found in the supply depot. The slight taste of petrol was masked with a drop of brandy.[19]

At 7.20 a.m., a full ten minutes before the main attack, a gigantic mine was detonated with 40,000 pounds of HE at the end of a long tunnel reaching under the German lines at the Hawthorn Ridge Redoubt. It was set then because the miners wanted ten minutes to repair possible defects in the fuses, and Lt.-Gen. Hunter-Weston thought that much time was needed to avoid falling debris‡ and for the 2nd Battalion Royal Fusiliers to get across no man's land, seize the high lip of the crater and

---

* There is no truth to the rumour that the Ulster Division was given double rations of rum.
† Or 'Blighty' as Great Britain was universally nicknamed.
‡ When a mine had been exploded near Fricourt back on 26 March, Maj. Probert recorded: 'At 6.20 a.m. one of our mines went up. I watched from the top of the hill. The noise made by the Germans who had been buried was heard all night. Flames from the explosion lasted in some cases twenty seconds.'[20]

lay down fire on the defenders to help the other attacking bat-talions.[21] In the event, however, those Germans who survived the initial explosion reached the rim of the huge crater first, and were able to set up their machine guns before the Royal Fusiliers arrived.

'The explosion was a signal for the infantry attack,' the war diary of the German 119th Reserve Regiment recorded, 'and everyone got ready and stood on the lower steps of the dugouts, rifles in hand, waiting for the bombardment to lift. In a few min-utes the shelling ceased, and we rushed up the steps and out into the crater positions. Ahead of us wave after wave of British troops were crawling out of their trenches and coming towards us at a walk, their bayonets glistening in the sun.'[22] The first three com-panies of the Royal Fusiliers were cut down in minutes.

THE HAWTHORN RIDGE MINE
40,000 pounds of High Explosive were detonated under the Hawthorn Ridge ten minutes before the attack.

Hunter-Weston's decision to blow the mine at 7.20 a.m. was a controversial one. 'There is no doubt to my mind that,' wrote Lt. Albert Whitlock of the 2nd Royal Fusiliers later, 'had this been timed for firing almost simultaneously with the attack, we should, in the general confusion, have been able to overrun the Redoubt with little or no opposition and thus stop the intense direct machine gun fire.' He believed that months of work by the Royal Engineers miners had been wasted because of an unnecessary ten-minute pause. Yet although some of the officers after the battle criticized 'a fatal error [which] gave the game away all along the line', saying that it 'prejudiced our chances of success considerably' and was even 'fatal to the success of the attack as a whole', the Germans were already fully alerted to the coming attack.[23] (Some men did move out into no man's land before the Hawthorn Mine exploded—including the 2nd South Wales Borderers, 1st Royal Inniskilling Fusiliers and the leading battalions of 94th Brigade.)[24]

Lochnagar Redoubt was a German strongpoint defended by 200 Württembergers south of La Boisselle, but unbeknownst to them there was a 1,400 yard-long (1,280 m) tunnel reaching under it, which had been started in Becourt Wood in November 1915. 'We were to stand at the bridge ready for the mine to blow', recalled Pte. Elliot of the 20th Battalion Northumberland Fusiliers (Tyneside Scottish) of the situation at 7.23 a.m. 'We had short ladders. Then someone called Now! Get out of the parapet boys, she's going up.'[25] At 7.28 a.m. the Royal Engineers' tunnelling companies blew up two mines at Y Sap, north of La Boisselle, which contained 40,000 lbs (18,000 kg) of HE, and the Lochnagar Mine which contained 60,000 lbs (27,000 kg), and left a crater 90 yards (82 m) wide and 70 (64 m) deep. Soil and stones rained down throughout the area.

'At Boisselle, the earth heaved and flashed,' recorded Cecil Day-Lewis, who was flying overheard when the mine was exploded, 'a tremendous and magnificent column rose into the sky. There was an ear-splitting roar, drowning out all the guns, flinging the machine sideways in the repercussing air. The earthy column rose higher and higher to almost four thousand feet (1,219 m).'[26] Although the Y Sap and Lochnagar Mines were on the outskirts of La Boisselle, when the 34th Division attacked two minutes later it failed to capture the fortified village, which did not fall for another three days.

Although the Germans had evacuated the area around Y

THE TYNESIDE IRISH
Going over the top from the Tara–Usna Line to attack La Boisselle on the morning of the 1 July.

Sap, having spotted the danger beforehand, they had no inkling about the Lochnagar Mine and many of their men were killed. Half of the 7th Company of the 110th Regiment were killed and the 2nd company was completely wiped out, as was the 5th company but for one NCO and 15 men.[27] Yet the survivors stayed at their posts and waited for the British attack. They crawled out onto the lip of the giant crater with their machine guns. Two brigades of Northumberland Fusiliers, the Tyneside Scottish and the Tyneside Irish were cut down; the Reserves were shot to pieces even before reaching their own front line. Because the communication trenches were full of wounded men getting back to safety, the attack of the Tyneside Reserve brigade had to take place in full view of the German machine guns, so the

34th Division took more casualties than any other unit that day, a truly appalling 6,380 in all.

In all five mines went up at 7.28 a.m. at various points along the front. 'Our infantry were also holding the eastern lip of the large newly formed crater', recorded an aviator above the Y Sap mine at La Boisselle. 'The fighting around the crater must have been very severe as dozens of bodies could be seen lying about outside [the] crater on the white chalk, and also inside [the] crater. And as shrapnel burst over the crater others could be seen rolling down the steep incline on the inside.'[28]

Lt.-Col. E. C. J. Minet of the 18th Division recalled sweating before Zero Hour, but put it down to nervous excitement.[29] 'For God's sake,' said a soldier in the 18th Division, 'let us get going.'[30] At 7.30 a.m. the barrage lifted and there was a brief moment of unexpected silence before the officers checked their watches,* ordered bayonets to be fixed and rifles loaded and then blew their whistles as the signal to go over the top. Four days earlier the order had gone out that, in order not to differentiate themselves for the benefit of snipers, 'All Officers should dress alike as the men as near as possible'.[31] They carried rifles as well as their Webley .455-in. revolvers, therefore, but they remained conspicuous because they led from the front, as casualty rates even higher than the Non-commissioned officers and other ranks eloquently attested.

Very often the junior subalterns were fresh from their public

---

* Which often had wire screens over the faces to prevent them from being smashed.

schools and universities.* On 3 and 4 August 1914, for example, twenty-two of England's best public school cricketers played in the annual schools match. By the end of the war seven of the twenty-two had been killed.[32] The popular (if inappropriate) phrase differentiating the leonine soldiers and donkey-like officers did not apply to the junior regimental officers, who put a good deal of thought into the tactics that would best defeat the enemy and preserve their men's lives. Capt. Duncan Martin of the 9th Devonshires, for example, made a plasticine model of the assault ground with which to explain the attack on Mametz to his company, though in the end it did not help as his command was destroyed by a single German machine gun in a corner of the civilian cemetery across the Vallée Martin (an ironic coincidence of names).

Another inventive captain, Wilfred 'Billy' Nevill of the 8th Royal East Surrey Regiment, bought four footballs while on leave and gave one to each of his platoons, offering a prize to the first one to kick one into the German trenches in front of Montauban. One platoon painted the words: 'The Great European Cup. The Final. East Surreys v The Bavarians. Kick-off at Zero. No referee' onto their ball. Sure enough, as one survivor recalled: 'As the gunfire died away, I saw an infantryman climb over the parapet into no man's land, beckoning others to follow. As he did so he kicked off a football; a good kick, the ball rose and travelled towards the German line. That seemed to be the signal to advance.'[33] No one collected the prize, however, as

---

* When Maj. Probert attended the Old Etonian dinner in the Hotel Godbert in Amiens on 4 June, there were 168 officers of the 4th Army present. They sang the school song, 'Carmen Etonense'.

Capt. Nevill was killed before he had covered 20 yards (18 m). His company Sgt.-Maj. C. Wills and Lt. R. G. Soames were also killed, but the men went on.[34] His idea has been ridiculed as making light of the operation, but in fact it was intended to raise morale and encourage forward movement, and was a good one. Among many other officers who distinguished themselves that day was Lt.-Col. Reginald Bastard, 2nd Lincolnshires, who crossed no man's land no fewer than four times to rally his troops.

Lt.-Col. Ambrose Ricardo, who commanded the County Tyrone Battalion in the 36th Division, recalled how his men advanced with 'no fuss, no shouting, no running: everything orderly, solid and thorough. Just like the men themselves. Here and there a boy would wave his hand at me as I shouted "Good luck!" to them through my megaphone, and all had a happy face. Many were carrying loads. Fancy advancing against heavy fire carrying a heavy roll of barbed wire on your shoulders!'[35] Yet in front of the Allies along the front were almost one thousand German machine gun posts, manned by brave and well-trained men.[36]* 'Now Jerry started,' recalled Pte. W. Senescall of the Cambridge Battalion. 'His machine guns let fly. Down they all went. I could see them dropping one after another as the gun swept along them.'[37]

'The English came walking, as though they were going to the theatre or as though they were on a parade ground,' recalled Uffz. Paul Scheytt of the 109th Reserve Infantry Regiment. 'We felt they were mad.'[38] Another recalled: 'We were very surprised

---

* Some German machine-gunners handcuffed themselves to their guns in sheer bravado – one was taken prisoner, another was killed.

to see them walking, we had never seen that before... They went down in their hundreds. You didn't have to aim, we just fired into them.' Musketier Karl Blenk of the 169th Regiment remembered changing the barrel of his machine gun five times, after firing 5,000 rounds each time. If the machine-gunner had an accurate ranging sight on the opposing trench, many of the men were killed even as they reached the top of the ladders. 'The German machine gun fire was terrible,' said Pte. W. Carter of the 1st Bradford Pals. 'Our Colonel was hit after only a few steps along the trench.'[39] Nor was it only machine gun and rifle fire that the Germans laid down: 'A whizzbang caught my platoon sergeant in the throat and his head disappeared', recalled Pte. J. Devennie of the Derry Volunteers.[40] It was carnage within moments, all along the British line. 'Five minutes after the

TAKING HOME THE SPOILS
German soldiers return to their trenches with captured
Allied Lewis guns on their shoulders.

attack started,' said Pte. J. F. Pout of the 55th Field Ambulance, 'if the British public could have seen the wounded struggling to get out of the line, the war would have possibly been stopped by public opinion.'[41]

Henry Williamson, who was later to write the celebrated nature story *Tarka the Otter*, recalled the feeling when the German machine guns opened up on the 8th Division attacking Ovillers: 'A steam-harsh noise filled the air. [I] knew what that was: machine gun bullets, each faster than sound, with its hiss and its air crack arriving almost simultaneously, many scores of thousands of bullets in the air together at the same time and coming from all directions.'[42] When men were hit, he wrote, 'Some seem to pause, with bowed heads, and sink carefully to their knees, and roll slowly over, and lie still. Others roll and roll, and scream and grip my legs in utmost fear, and I have to struggle to break away, while the dust and earth on my tunic changes from grey to red... who could have imagined that the "Big Push" was going to be like this?'[43] Yet in every single brigade and battalion, the men marched on. The 94th Brigade of 31st Division, for example, 'advanced in line after line, as if on parade', as its commanding officer Brig. H. C. Rees recalled, 'and not a man shirked going through the extremely heavy barrage, or facing the machine gun and rifle fire that finally wiped them out... hardly a man of ours got to the German front line.'[44] Where the wire had been cut the men were funnelled together, 'and it was there those patterned criss-cross streams of bullets caught us.'[45]

The German 180th Regiment in the Ovillers sector, facing the onslaught of the 8th Division, lost 78 killed and 108 wounded in the preliminary bombardment and its front defences were damaged, as were those of the 110th Regiment. Nonetheless the survivors knew how vital it was to reach the parapet. A soldier from that unit was later to write an account of this whose clarity and immediacy justifies extensive quotation:

> The intense bombardment was realized by all to be the prelude to an infantry assault sooner or later. The men in the dugouts therefore waited ready, belts full of hand grenades around them, gripping their rifles and waiting for the bombardment to lift from the front defence zone onto the rear defences. It was of vital importance not to lose a second in taking up position in the open to meet the British infantry which would advance immediately behind the artillery barrage. Looking towards the British trenches through the long trench periscopes held up out of the dugout entrances there could be seen a mass of steel helmets above the parapet showing that the storm troops were ready for an assault. At 7.30 a.m. the hurricane of shells ceased as suddenly as it had begun. Our men at once clambered up the steep shafts leading from the dugouts to daylight and ran singly or in groups to the nearest shell craters. The machine guns were pulled out of the dugouts and hurriedly placed in position, their crews dragging the heavy ammunition boxes up the steps and out to the guns. A rough firing line was thus rapidly established. As soon as the men were in position a series of extended lines of infantry were seen moving forward from the British trenches. The first line appeared to continue without end to right and left. It was followed quickly by a second line, then a third and fourth. They came on at a steady easy pace as if expecting to find nothing alive in

our front trenches. Some appeared to be carrying kodaks [cameras] to perpetuate the memory of their triumphal march across the German defences.* The front line, preceded by a thin line of skirmishers and bombers, was now half way across no man's land. 'Get ready!' was now passed across our front from crater to crater, and heads appeared over the crater edge as final positions were taken for the best view, and machine guns mounted firmly in place. A few moments later, when the leading British line was within a hundred yards, the rattle of machine gun and rifle fire broke out along the whole line of shell-holes. Some fired kneeling so as to get a better target over the broken ground, whilst others, in their excitement, stood up regardless of their own safety, to fire into the crowd of men in front of them. Red rockets flew up into the blue sky as a signal to the artillery, and immediately afterwards a mass of shell from the German batteries tore through the air and burst among the advancing lines. Whole sections seemed to fall and the rear formations, moving in closer order, quickly scattered. The advance rapidly crumbled under this hail of shell and bullets. All along the line men could be seen throwing up their arms and collapsing never to move again… The British soldier, however, has no lack of courage, and once his hand is set to the plough he is not easily turned from his purpose. The extended lines, though badly shaken and with many gaps, now came on all the faster. Instead of a leisurely walk they covered the ground in short rushes at the double. Within a few minutes the leading troops had advanced to within a stone's throw of our front trench, and whilst some of us continued to fire at point-blank range, others

---

* Almost certainly these were gas mask boxes, not cameras.

threw hand grenades among them. The British bombers
answered back, whilst the infantry rushed forward with
fixed bayonets. The noise of battle became indescribable.
The shouting of orders and the shrill cheers as the British
charged forward could be heard above the violent and
intense fusillade of machine guns and rifles and bursting
bombs, and above the deep thunderings of the artillery
and shell explosions. With all this were mingled the
moans and groans of the wounded, the cries for help and
the last screams of death. Again and again the extended
lines of British infantry broke against the German
defence like waves against a cliff, only to be beaten back.
It was an amazing spectacle of unexampled gallantry,
courage and bulldog determination on both sides.[46]

The 180th Regiment lost only 83 men killed, 184 wounded and
13 missing that whole day, most of them in the preliminary bombardment rather than the infantry assault.

The distances the men had to go across no man's land varied widely from sector to sector, and also within sectors. At the
Glory Hole* at La Boisselle, the two front lines were closer
than anywhere else in the whole Western Front, a matter of
only 100 feet (30 m), so there was constant mining and counter-
mining. Professional coal miners from Cornwall, Wales, Yorkshire, Northumberland, Nottinghamshire and Durham did vital
work underground. The Norwich Engineers in 34th Division
cleared much of the wire the night before the attack. In some
places covered by the 29th Division, for example, opposite the
Sunken Road and Hawthorn crater, no man's land was only

* The ironic name given by the Tommies to a very dangerous 'hot spot'; known
as *Ilôt* in French and *Granatof* – 'Grenade Alley' – in German.

200 to 250 yards (183 to 229 m) wide, whereas there were places nearby where it was twice or even thrice that.[46] The 16th Middlesex had to cover 400 yards (366 m), and the right flank of the 2nd South Wales Borderers 700 (640 m). To march even 200 yards (183 m) at walking pace would take four minutes, in which time a single German machine gun could fire well over fifteen hundred rounds, and have time to reload several times.

Yet a deliberate decision had been taken by the High Command not to dig trenches much closer to the enemy than 200 yards (183 m), as the senior operational planner on the staff of 29th Division, Lt.-Col. C. G. Fuller, told the official war historians after the war: 'About a month before the attack, the whole question had been discussed by the Commander-in-Chief (Haig), Chief of the General Staff (Major-General Sir Launcelot Kiggell), Fourth Army (Rawlinson), VIII Corps (Hunter-Weston) and 29th Division (De Lisle) commanders in conference and they had come to the conclusion that it was undesirable to dig trenches closer to the Germans as it would make them realise that we intended to attack.'[48] Yet the Germans knew perfectly well that an attack was about to take place at the end of the seven-day bombardment, which Haig and the other senior officers present must have suspected.

'No man in his right mind would have done what we were doing', recalled LCpl. J. Cousins, of the 7th Bedfords.[49] 'To us they had to be killed. Kill or be killed. You are not normal.'[50] The reason that people continued moving forward rather than succumbing to the temptation (and natural human reaction) of flinging themselves onto the ground immediately was that they wanted to do right by the units on either side of them, whose

GERMAN HEAVY ARTILLERY
*German gunners loading a 24cm long-range
gun on the Somme.*

successes they were told were central to victory. No one wanted
to be in the unit that compromised the breakthrough. 'There
were no signs of cowardice, or "low morale" as we call it more
kindly, in those early days of the struggle', wrote the journalist
Philip Gibbs. As for the Germans, 'They fought with a desperate courage, holding on to positions in rearguard actions when
our guns were slashing them, and when our men were getting
near to them making us pay a heavy price for every little copse
or gully or section of trench, and above all serving their machine
guns at La Boisselle, Ovillers, above Fricourt, round Contalmaison, and at all points of their gradual retreat, with a splendid
obstinacy until they were killed or captured.'[51]

It was untrue that there were no signs of cowardice at all, or
'lack of moral fibre' as it came to be called (and still later, more

humanely, post-traumatic stress disorder). When one of Siegfried Sassoon's brother officers could not move himself out of
the dugout, 'We left Jenkins* crouching in a corner, where he
remained for most of the day. His haggard blinking face haunts
my memory. He was an example of the paralyzing effect which
such an experience could produce on a nervous system sensitive to noise.' Although at the time Sassoon felt no sympathy
for him, by 1930, once he had the chance to reflect on the effects
of trauma, he did.† Although British colonels did have the
legal 'sanction' of summary execution to prevent unit collapse
through panic during battle, none of them had to resort to such
drastic measures at any time on the Somme, where overall the
courage shown was exemplary. As Winston Churchill put it in
his history of the First World War, *The World Crisis*, 'If two or
ten lives were required by their Commanders to kill one German, no word of complaint ever rose from the fighting troops.
No attack, however forlorn, however fatal, found them without
ardour... Martyrs not less than soldiers, they fulfilled the high
purpose of duty with which they were imbued. The battlefields
of the Somme were the graveyards of Kitchener's Army.'[52]

Only 634 Victoria Crosses were awarded during the First
World War, one for every 14,000 British and Commonwealth
soldiers mobilized, which a recent historian states was 'a parsi-
monious rate of distribution compared to the relative largesse of
the nineteenth century'.[53]‡ The nine men who won the Victoria

* Not his real name.
† If Jenkins had been a private rather than an officer, he would almost certainly
have been court-martialled, with a very high chance of being given the death
penalty, but there was only an 11 per cent chance of this being carried out.
‡ The total includes one for the American Unknown Soldier interred at Arlington.

Cross (VC) for their actions on the Somme on 1 July 1916 were Capt. E. N. F. Bell of the 9th Royal Inniskilling Fusiliers, Lt. Geoffrey Cather, adjutant of the 9th Royal Irish Fusiliers, Capt. John

CAPTAIN ERIC BELL VC
An artist's impression of the courage shown by Captain Eric Bell, which won him the Victoria Cross, one of nine awarded on the first day of the Somme.

Green of the Royal Army Medical Corps, Maj. Stewart Loudon-Shand of the 10th Yorkshires (Green Howards), Pte. W. F. McFadzean of the 14th Royal Irish Rifles, Rifleman Robert Quigg of the 12th Royal Irish Rifles, Drummer Walter Ritchie of the 2nd Seaforth Highlanders, Cpl. G. Sanders of the 1/7th West Yorkshires and Sgt. James Turnbull of the 17th Highland Light Infantry. Of these nine, three survived the war, three are buried in military cemeteries at Foncquevillers, Bécordel-Bécourt and Authuille, and three have no known graves.[54] Illustrating how extraordinary heroism was not confined to any specific army rank, the nine comprise two privates, a drummer, a corporal, a sergeant, a lieutenant, two captains and a major. In all, fifty-one VCs were awarded during the Somme battle; twenty to junior officers, twelve to NCOs and nineteen to privates, one-third of them posthumous.[55]

Lt. Cather won his VC at Beaumont Hamel when he was the only surviving officer of his battalion. Between 7 p.m. and midnight on 1 July, he went out onto no man's land with other volunteers to recover three wounded men. The next morning he rescued a fourth man and delivered water to others, while under constant machine gun and intermittent artillery fire. He died later that morning, and won a posthumous VC, even though back in December 1914 Haig had ruled out the award of VCs merely for saving the wounded. The reason Cather was honoured, according to a recent book on the internal politics of the award, was that—as well as showing 'the most conspicuous bravery', as his citation put it—'In the days that followed the start of the Battle of the Somme, Haig needed all the "good" publicity that could be mustered; in the absence of obvious battlefield victory, dead heroes were the best means of garnering the sympathy of a critical press and a variously bewildered and appalled general public.'[56] Because so much heroism was shown in the first months of the war, the Military Cross (MC) had been invented in December 1914, partly as a way of keeping the VC rare and difficult to obtain. In the course of the war, more than 37,000 MCs were awarded, almost three thousand of them with bars (that is, a second award). In April 1916 the Military Medal (MM) was founded for other ranks.

Another of the VCs from the first day of the offensive was awarded to the twenty-one-year-old Pte. Billy McFadzean, who had shown 'most conspicuous bravery' in a closely packed trench at Thiepval Wood. A specialist bomber, he was ordered to unpack grenades while under heavy German shelling, but he dropped the box and two grenades fell on the ground with their pins knocked out. McFadzean threw himself onto them, dying instantly but saving everyone else in the trench except one man who lost a leg. 'He well knew his danger,' read the citation in the *London Gazette*, 'but without a moment's hesitation he gave his life for his comrades.'[57] (The War Office paid for the railway ticket for McFadzean's father to go from Belfast to London to receive the VC from King George V at Buckingham Palace, but he was made to travel third class.)

'When I got near the German trenches I could see some of them coming out with their hands up,' recalled LCpl. W. Sanders of the 10th Essex Regiment, 'but, when they saw how many of us had been hit, they changed their minds and ran back again.'[58] In those places where the British did capture enemy positions, they found that the Germans had many more communication trenches, so their efforts to extend right and left were limited by the sheer size of the German entrenching system.[59] By 8.30 a.m. just under half of the 66,000 British soldiers who had attacked in 84 battalions were casualties, at the rate since Zero Hour of 500 a minute, or more than eight per second.[60] By noon, 100,000 men and 129 battalions had been committed to the battle, but by 3 p.m. so few gains had been made that the cavalry was ordered to stand down, as they would not be needed to exploit break-throughs in the line.[61] Until that point, the cavalrymen had been standing close to their fully-laden mounts waiting for the order to advance.

Instead, stretcher-bearers were sent out to try to bring in the wounded, many of whom were fired on by the Germans. Max Plowman started the war as a member of the Territorial Army Field Ambulance Corps in 1914, though he later became a commissioned officer (and, before the war's end, a conscientious objector). He recalled one of the stretcher-bearers on 1 July called Side, who that day 'carried stretchers under fire continuously for twenty-four hours. Anyone who knows the weight of a loaded stretcher and remembers the heat, the condition of the ground, and what the firing was like upon that day, will agree with me that the Victoria Cross would have expressed rather less than Side's deserts.'[62] However all Side received was a promotion to corporal.

Once they were back in the British trenches, the wounded survivors were not out of trouble. Sgt.-Maj. Ernest Shephard of the 1st Dorsets wrote in his diary that it was 'A lovely day, intensely hot'. Born in Lyme Regis in 1892, the son of a photographer who was to lose two of his three sons in the war, Shephard had enlisted in the part-time Special Reserve in 1909 but joined the Dorset Regiment later that year and was a sergeant by 1914. His diary entry continues:

> Lots of casualties in my trench. The enemy are enfilading us with heavy shell, dropping straight on us. A complete trench mortar battery of men killed by one shell, scores of dead and badly wounded in trench, now 1 p.m. Every move we make brings intense fire, as trenches so badly battered the enemy can see all our movements. Lot of wounded in front we got in, several were hit again and killed in trench. We put as many wounded as possible in best spots in trench and I sent a lot down [i.e. down the line to casualty clearing stations or advanced dressing stations], but I had so many of my own men killed and wounded that after a time I could not do this. Sent urgent messages to Brigade asking for RAMC bearers to be sent to evacuate wounded but none came although Brigade said they had been dispatched. Meanwhile the enemy deliberately shelled the wounded between the trenches with shrapnel, thus killing, or wounding again, most of them.[63]

At 3 p.m., once the Manchesters had gone through a sap and made an assault on the Leipzig Redoubt, brigade sent Shephard a message saying the 1st Dorsets—who now numbered a mere fifty-three men from B and C companies—would be relieved by the 15th Highland Light Infantry (HLI) as soon as possible. 'Meanwhile we were to hold tight. We needed to; literally we were blown from place to place. Men very badly shaken. As far as possible we cleared trenches of debris and dead. These we piled in heaps, enemy shells pitching on them made matters worse.' With the wounded 'suffering agonies', Shephard collected water bottles from the dead for them, before renewed shelling hit at 8 p.m. 'I had miraculous escapes', he wrote.[64] The HLI arrived to relieve him, but not until midnight.* Shephard was commissioned in November and killed two months later commanding a company of the Dorsets.

Behind the lines, estimates of the battle continued to be over-optimistic. 'During the day hundreds of German prisoners and our own wounded were passing through our lines,' recorded Gwilym Ewart Davies of the Royal Artillery:

> We have advanced much further than we expected to...
> Our wounded soldiers returning from the trenches
> were in excellent spirits. They were saying that as long
> as they had done what they were asked to do they didn't
> care about their wounds. They were, of course, no doubt
> glad that they were returning to England or 'Blighty' as
> they call it. Several of our chaps had souvenirs from the
> German prisoners, such as postcards, etc., but as I was
> on gun I was unable to get any... Our battery was firing
> about every three minutes... Without any exaggeration
> the roads were like the streets of London, so very busy
> were they.[65]

We are fortunate to be able to view the German experience of the Somme through the eyes of one of the greatest German novelists of the twentieth century, Ernst Jünger, who volunteered on

---

* When he knew his position was helpless, he ordered the supporting company to fall back in order not to be overwhelmed themselves, an action the military historian Richard Holmes has described as characteristically professional.

the opening day of the war in August 1914 and served throughout the conflict, becoming the country's youngest winner of its
highest valour award, the *Pour le Mérite*. A lieutenant in the Rifle
Regiment of Prince Albrecht of Prussia (the 73rd Hanoverian
Regiment), his autobiography *Stahlgewittern* (*Storm of Steel*),
first published in 1920, is one of the great books of the war, whatever one might think of his subsequent ultra-conservative/
quasi-Fascist politics. Jünger was based with his regiment
at Douchy-lès-Ayette to the north of what was to become the
Somme battlefield, and spent much of his time there and in
the front line at nearby Monchy-au-Bois. A few excerpts from
his trench diary from October 1915 show how dangerous and
uncomfortable it was long before the Allied offensive there the
following summer:

> 7 OCTOBER: In the morning, the sentry on our left flank was
> shot through both cheekbones. The blood spurted out
> of him in thick gouts. And, to cap it all, when Lieutenant
> von Ewald, visiting our sector to take pictures of Sap 'N'
> barely fifty yards (46 m) away, turned to climb down from
> the outlook, a bullet shattered the back of his skull and
> he died on the spot. Large fragments of skull were left
> littering the sentry platform.

> 19 OCTOBER: The middle platoon's section of trench was
> attacked with 6-in. shells. One man was hurled against a
> post by the blast so hard that he sustained serious internal
> injuries, and a splinter of wood punctured the arteries
> of his arm... That night, two men were wounded while
> unspooling wire.

> 30 OCTOBER: Following a torrential downpour in the night,
> all the traverses came down and formed a grey sludgy

porridge with the rain, turning the trench into a deep swamp. Our only consolation was that the British were just as badly off as we were, because we could see them baling out for all they were worth. Since our position has a little more elevation than theirs, we even managed to pump our excess their way... The crumpled trenches exposed a line of bodies left there from the previous autumn's fighting.[66]

Jünger wrote of how they blew the heads off pheasants—which with Teutonic humour they nicknamed 'cookpot volunteers' —caught rats with steel traps and then finished them off with clubs, and went out and collected unexploded shells, 'little ones and big ones, some weighing a hundredweight or more, all in plentiful supply', which underlines British complaints about the quality of the British ordnance.[67]

'Throughout the war,' he wrote, 'it was always my endeavour to view my opponent without animus, and to form an opinion of him as a man on the basis of the courage he showed. I would always try to seek him out in combat and kill him, and I expected nothing else from him. But never did I entertain mean thoughts of him. When prisoners fell into my hands later on, I felt responsible for their safety and would always do everything in my power for them.'[68]

Although a great deal has been written about the Christmas Truce of 1914, where Tommy and Fritz fraternized, exchanged cigarettes and played football in no man's land, Jünger makes it clear that there was no repeat of this the following year. 'We sang hymns,' he recalled, 'to which the British responded with machine gun fire. On Christmas Day we lost one man to a ricochet in the head. Immediately afterwards, the British attempted a friendly gesture by hauling a Christmas tree up on their traverse, but our angry troops quickly shot it down again, to which Tommy replied with rifle grenades. It was all in all a less than merry Christmas.'[69]

By early March, Jünger reported, they had seen the worst of the mud and as the weather dried, the trench solidified. Time was spent in digging deep, thirty-one-step dugouts in the chalk and clay, linked by underground passages so that they could cross 'from right to left of our frontage in safety and comfort'. His favourite project was a 60-yard (55 m) underground passage linking his dugout with the company commander's, 'with other dormitories and munitions depots off to either side'. It was far better than anything the British had at that time, and as Jünger pointed out, 'All this was to come in handy in the fighting to come'.[70] For they were under no illusions as to what was coming; on 16 June their general warned them in a speech that a large-scale offensive was to be expected soon. Four days later, Jünger was ordered to eavesdrop on the British line to find out if they were mining underneath his own trenches, and he left a vivid account of what such an expedition in no man's land felt like: 'These moments of nocturnal prowling leave an indelible impression', he wrote:

> Eyes and ears are tensed to the maximum, the rustling approach of strange feet in the tall grass is an unutterably menacing thing. Your breath comes in shallow bursts; you have to force yourself to stifle any panting or wheezing. There is a little mechanical click as the safety-catch of your pistol is taken off; the sound cuts straight through

your nerves. Your teeth are grinding on the fuse-pin of
your hand grenade. The encounter will be short and
murderous. You tremble with two contradictory impulses:
the heightened awareness of the huntsman, and the terror
of the quarry.[71]

In the fortnight leading up to 1 July 1916 there were so many
mortar attacks that Jünger recalled always walking along the
trenches 'one eye aloft, and the other on the entrance of the
nearest deep dugout… Occasionally my ears were utterly deafened by a single fiendish crashing burst of flame. Then incessant hissing gave me the sense of hundreds of pound weights
rushing down at incredible speed, one after the other. Or a dud
shell landed with a short, heavy ground-shaking thump. Shrapnel burst by the dozen, like dainty crackers, shook loose their
little balls in a dense cloud, and the empty casings rasped after
they were gone. Each time the shells landed anywhere close, the
earth flew up and down, and metal shards drove themselves into
it.'[72] He had used his gas mask case to carry his sandwiches in
before he saw some men who had been gassed, 'pressing their
hands against their sides and groaning and retching while their
eyes watered… a few of them went on to die over the next several days, in terrible agony.' Thereafter he used it for his gas-
mask only, and he took it with him wherever he went.

Jünger was stationed behind the lines on 1 July, and his regiment only lost forty men in the engagement which 'left plenty of
dead on our wires'. Burying the coffins, 'with their names written in pencil on the unplaned planks', the minister began with
the words: 'Gibraltar, that is your motto, and why not, for have

you not stood firm like the rock in the sea surge!'* For all that burying his comrades had been 'a sorry task', Jünger and the survivors felt perfectly able to celebrate that night 'the success of the engagement with several well-earned bottles'.[73] As well they might, for the British army had suffered the worst one-day losses in its history, and for terribly few territorial gains, most of which were short lived.

---

* Jünger's Hanoverian regiment dated back to the days of King George III and they loyally served their (Anglo-German) Elector by defending Gibraltar against the Spanish and French through the great siege of 1779–83. In the First World War this regiment wore the name 'Gibraltar' embroidered on the cuffs of their jackets, which was rather confusing for Tommies when they captured them.

FIVE

THE FIRST
OF JULY

'It was about this time that
my feeling of confidence was replaced
by an acceptance of the fact
that I had been sent here to die.'[1]

PTE. J. CROSSLEY,
15th Durham Light Infantry

'THE ATTACK IS TO GO IN TOMORROW MORNING AT 7.30,' Gen. Sir Douglas Haig had written to his wife on 30 June 1916, 'I feel that everything possible for us to do to achieve success has been done. But whether or not we are successful lies in the Power above. But *I do feel* that in my plans I have been helped by a Power that is not my own. So I am easy in my mind and ready to do my best whatever happens tomorrow.'[2] Yet everything possible had certainly not been done to achieve success, and from the north to the south of the battlefield, the fortunes of the Allied divisions on 1 July 1916 varied greatly as they attacked the nine fortified towns, thirteen redoubts and their connecting trench lines. Generally speaking, their fortunes improved the further south they launched their assault. In the most northerly sector, at Gommecourt, the 46th and 56th Divisions' sacrificial diversion was an unmitigated disaster. The 31st, 4th and 29th Divisions suffered badly at Serre and Beaumont Hamel. To their south, the 32nd and 36th Divisions were thrown back at Thiepval, although some short-term gains were made. At the central axis of the attack, the 8th and 34th Divisions also made little or no progress against Ovillers and La Boisselle. Further south still, the 21st and 7th Divisions had some partial success around Fricourt and captured Mametz, though at a very high price in blood, while the 18th and 30th Divisions took their objectives around and including Montauban. Below Montauban, on both banks of the Somme itself, the French army was very successful, taking all its objectives.

In the northern sector, two divisions of VII Corps of the 3rd Army, commanded by Lt.-Gen. Sir Thomas D'Oyly 'Snowball' Snow, attacked Gommecourt, hoping to eliminate a German bulge (or 'salient') in the line but also to create a diversion that would draw German reserves away from the real place at which Haig intended to break through, which was further south between Thiepval and Pozières. The wood and village of Gommecourt were part of the Kern Redoubt, an immensely strong defensive position with 360-degree views of the land around it, so it should probably not have been attacked at all, and certainly not in such huge numbers considering it was only ever intended as a diversion.

The north of Gommecourt was assaulted by the 18,000-strong 46th (North Midland) Division, which had been created out of the part-time soldiers of the Territorial forces from Staffordshire, Derbyshire, Nottinghamshire, Leicestershire and Lincolnshire and had landed in France in March 1915 under the command of Maj.-Gen. the Hon. E. J. Stuart-Wortley, who had previously served in South Africa. In the Battle of Loos it had lost 3,500 men attempting unsuccessfully to capture the Hohenzollern Redoubt, partly due to bad cooperation between the divisional artillery and infantry.

They trained for the attack on Gommecourt with trenches dug to resemble the German lines, but in the ten days before 1 July the division was fully occupied holding the front-line trenches, and was shelled regularly. For the fortnight prior to the attack, recalled Cpl. E. J. Lawson of the 1/7th Sherwood Foresters, 'we rarely had a stitch of dry clothing'. On being told the attack was about to take place, he wrote, 'We felt a great sense of relief although in anything but a fit state to undertake so mammoth a task.'[3]

Haig directed that the German trench in front of the 46th Division should not be shelled, but only the support and reserve trenches, as he wanted the front trench to be kept intact for use by the division once it was captured.[4] To make matters worse, when they went over the top the men found the barbed wire largely intact, and the smoke barrage that had been laid down to confuse the Germans had hidden the few places where there were gaps in the wire. The first German trench was just in front of the wood, 300 yards (274 m) from the British lines. A few dozen men got through the small gaps in the wire but were killed in the attempt, while the vast majority were cut down in the field between Gommecourt Wood and what is today the Gommecourt Wood New Cemetery.

German artillery as well as machine guns destroyed the 5th and 6th Battalions of the North Staffordshires and the 5th and 6th Battalions of the South Staffordshires, which is why a large number of the North and South Staffordshire graves in the cemetery are not identified by name. Once the 46th Division's advance collapsed, the Germans concentrated on repelling the 56th Division to the south of Gommecourt, and by 9.30 a.m. it was back in its own trenches having taken a mammoth 4,300 casualties, against 2,455 for the 46th. Although Stuart-Wortley had suffered the fewest losses of any of the British generals, he was relieved of his command two days later. (Haig had long rubbed up badly against him, and was quick to agree to Lt.-Gen. Sir Thomas D'Oyly Snow's request that he be sacked immediately.)

Haig managed to add grave insult to the injury already caused by then blackening the name of the 46th in his war diary, writing: 'The Gommecourt attack was also progressing well. 46th Division had [the] northern corner of Gommecourt Wood… But eventually [the] right brigade of 46th Division did not press on.'[5] This is totally unfair, as the large numbers of dead from the 137th Brigade in the Gommecourt Wood New Cemetery silently attest. They had pressed on as far as their losses could possibly allow. Cpl. Lawson was hit even before getting out of the trench. 'Just as we were signalled', he recalled, 'a shrapnel shell burst a few feet over the top of the trench, and I received a shrapnel bullet in the back.' It probably saved his life. Although the divisional artillery commander later claimed to have cut the

A BIRD'S EYE VIEW
An aerial photograph of the south end of Gommecourt village and park, showing the destruction caused by the fighting, October 1916.

wire 'along the whole front for a distance of 1,500 yards (1,372 m)', he was wrong. 'I advanced with the first wave and got as far as the wire,' recalled Sgt. H. Fitzgerald of the 1/6th North Staffordshires, 'which was very thick and not cut. We couldn't get through.' Whereupon the enemy had opened up with machine gun fire.[6]

Attacking Gommecourt from the south was Maj.-Gen. C.P.A. Hull's 56th (London) Division, which included the Rangers, London Scottish and London Rifle Brigade. The Londoners found the wire cut in several places and overran the first two lines of trenches but were held up at the third, as well as at Nameless Farm. The division then came under heavy German artillery attack out in the open, which prevented reinforcements reaching them across no man's land. When the Germans began their counter-attack, therefore, the Londoners could not defend their gains. For all that a bombing section of the Queen's Westminster Rifles got behind Gommecourt, it proved impossible for the 56th to join up with the 46th. Although the attack on Gommecourt had been purely diversionary, it was of course impossible for the General Staff to tell that to the divisions concerned, so support battalions were sent into the fray and were also destroyed. 'Guns of all calibres pounded their system of trenches till it looked for all the world like nothing more than a ploughed field', wrote an officer of the 56th Division.[7]

Cpl. Sidney Appleyard recalled how according to one report that his unit received, 'Gommecourt Wood had been knocked to the ground and the Germans had evacuated the whole position'.[8] But it was yet another over-optimistic report, a rumour.

'Line after line advanced and disappeared in the clouds of smoke, and on several occasions one could see batches of men disappear as a shell exploded in their midst', he later wrote. 'On we went and it seemed marvellous how the pieces missed us, for the air appeared to be alive with missiles. At last after advancing about thirty yards (27.4 m) I was struck in the thigh by a bullet, the force of which knocked me over. The only thing to do was to crawl back, and this I did... Knowing that a good number had been hit, I decided to crawl out on top again and give any assistance that might be required. My efforts were useless for the only man left out there had been shot through the head and killed instantly.'[9] He crawled to an ambulance station at Sailly, from where he was sent to Le Tréport hospital, from which he wrote the next day: 'The doctors and nurses are very kind to us all and it is worth getting wounded. The weather is glorious and it is a treat to get away from the booming of the guns.'[10] He was proud of what they had achieved: 'The London Territorials were outnumbered and beaten, but by no means disgraced, for under such conditions we did remarkably well in taking the first two lines, and if we had been in the position to get reserves up we should certainly have reached our objective.'[11]

Despite taking their first objectives in places where the wire had been well cut, the men of the 56th Division were forced back into their own trenches by the end of the day. The *Official History* was damning of Haig for ordering a major attack at Gommecourt at all. 'The VII Corps before Gommecourt, having played its part in the preparatory period by attracting an extra enemy division,' Edmonds wrote, 'the assault... at that spot should have been countermanded by GHQ order.'[12] It further pointed out that 'Any chance of surprise which existed on the front between Fricourt and Gommecourt was lost by the enemy overhearing at La Boisselle a British telephone message and the firing of the mine at Hawthorn Ridge ten minutes before zero.'[13]

At Gommecourt Wood New Cemetery lies LCpl. Daniel George McMillan, twenty-three years old, from the 14th Battalion London Regiment (London Scottish). He was the son of Alexander and Margaret McMillan of East London, South Africa, who chose this inscription for his gravestone: 'He died for King and Country and the freedom of the world.' Nearby lies Pte. G. H. Saltinstall, aged nineteen, of the North Staffordshire Regiment, son of a widowed mother from Burton-on-Trent, who chose the words: 'Death divides but memory clings.' In Gommecourt British Cemetery No. 2 is buried Cpl. Leonard Edward Rowe, twenty years old, from the 2nd Battalion London Regiment (Royal Fusiliers). He came from Clapham and was, his headstone records, 'A mere boy but a great sportsman'. A Star of David is on a grave believed to be that of 2nd Lt. J. Josephs, aged nineteen, from the 12th Battalion London Regiment (The Rangers), the son of David and Sabine Josephs of Willesden Lane, London.

To the south of the 56th Division was the 48th Division, which did not attack at all on 1 July. Once the Germans realized that they need not expect an attack in the sector north of Serre, they turned their guns there onto the 56th Division and Maj.-Gen. Robert Wanless O'Gowan's 31st Division to the south. The latter was made up of Pals battalions from northern English industrial towns such as Accrington, Bradford, Leeds, Barnsley and

Halifax. They were supposed to capture Serre and then protect the 4th Army from a counter-attack from the north. Attacking uphill from copses named after the four evangelists, they marched into a storm of 74,000 rounds of machine gun and rifle rounds, gaining little ground at huge expense.[14] Just off the Serre Road a single machine-gunner (named Kaiser) virtually destroyed the entire battalion of 11th East Lancashires (Accrington Pals).

The attack from Mark Copse of the 11th Battalion East Lancashire Regiment also failed within a few minutes. At 7.33 a.m. the 1st Barnsley Pals got up, dressed their line, walked forward the 300 yards (274 m) to the enemy line and were annihilated. The Accrington Pals suffered 585 casualties, the Sheffield Pals 512, the 1st Barnsley Pals 286 and the 2nd Barnsley Pals 275. By 7.50 a.m., after only seventeen minutes, the attack had completely failed. The Durham Light Infantry reached Pendant Copse 1¼ miles (2 km) in, and some Accrington Pals and Sheffield City Battalion reached Serre itself, but they could not hold the position. In all, the division lost over 3,600 men. 'I felt sick at the sight of this carnage and remember weeping', recalled LCpl. H. Bury of the Accrington Pals.[15] Of the Sheffield City Pals' battalion, the novelist John Harris in *Covenant with Death* wrote memorable words that describe many of the battalions of Kitchener's New Army on that summer day: 'Two years in the making. Ten minutes in the destroying. That was our history.'[16] It was said that no house in Accrington was left unaffected when the news of the Pals battalion's fate reached the town.[17]

In the Railway Hollow Cemetery, Pte. J. H. Mawdsley, of the East Lancashire Regiment has a gravestone that says, in the words of his wife Hetty from Clayton-le-Moors, Accrington, 'I have fought a good fight. Kept the faith. Finished the course.' In Serre Road No. 1 Cemetery Horace Iles of the 16th Battalion West Yorkshire Regiment is buried; he was the son of Elizabeth Iles of Spenceley Street, Leeds. His sister Florrie had written to him begging him to come home as he had lied about his age when volunteering and was only fourteen years old. The letter was returned with the words 'Killed in Action' stamped on it. In the Railway Hollow Cemetery, Pte. Archie Brammer, who died at twenty-two in the 12th Battalion Yorkshire and Lancashire Regiment (Sheffield City Battalion) has a headstone whose words were chosen by his parents, Mr W. H. and Mrs A. Brammer of Walkley, Sheffield: 'To live in hearts of those we love is not to die.'

To the right of the 31st Division was the Hon. Sir William Lambton's Regular 4th Division, whose objective was to capture the Quadrilateral Redoubt. This they managed to achieve but nothing more, because of what was happening on both their flanks. Under attack by German units from both Serre and Beaumont Hamel, they were forced to abandon the Quadrilateral the next morning, with total losses of 4,700.[18] Requests for renewed bombardments were hard to make as telephone lines were often cut by the barrage, and runners were often too late to make a difference. Generals could no longer control their men once they were in no man's land, or even stay in touch with them effectively. Those units that took the initiative and ran at the German trenches, such as the 1st Rifle Brigade, had far more of a chance of achieving their objectives.[19]

Just outside Serre Road Cemetery No. 2 is a memorial to Valentine Braithwaite, son of Sir Walter Braithwaite, who had been awarded one of the earliest MCs of the Battle of Mons and then served at Gallipoli. He had returned to France with the Somerset Light Infantry of the 4th Division and was killed on 1 July along with his colonel, his adjutant and four other officers. His body was not found. 'God buried him and no man knoweth his sepulcher', wrote his family on a simple cross.

To the south of the 4th Division was the 29th Division, whose plan was to advance from what is known as 'the Sunken Road' through the German positions for 2½ miles (4 km).[20] The 86th and 87th Brigades planned to capture the German front-line trenches in front of Beaumont Hamel at 7.30 a.m. and then at 8.30 a.m. the 88th Brigade, which included the Newfoundland Regiment, would move through them to attack the second line of German defences. Of this attack, Maj. James Ball of the Battery of the Royal Horse Artillery later wrote: 'To expect infantry to walk across 800 hundred yards [732 m] with full equipment, carrying... duckboards in the face of a fully armed enemy was to invite the massacre that actually occurred.'[21]

Unfortunately, the guns of the divisional artillery, which ought to have been bringing fire down on the German front trenches once it was clear that the attacks in the north had failed, were following the rigid timetable set out in the schedule, whereby they moved their fire forward by 100 yards (91 m) every two minutes. This meant that when the 29th Division was stopped in its tracks in no man's land in front of the Y Ravine at Beaumont Hamel, the barrage that should have been

'WE NEED FEAR NOTHING'
Newfoundland soldiers waiting in the St John's Road
support trench on July 1, 1916.

supporting it was instead shelling the opposite side of the valley, with no means of calling it back. 'Seldom have the evils of an inflexible, predetermined schedule of artillery fire been so tragically demonstrated', wrote the historian of the Newfoundland Regiment.[22] Communications between infantry, observers and artillery were still rudimentary, and so exact a science as moving a barrage forward in coordination with infantry movement was still impossible in mid-1916. Instead, timetables were used which worked for the artillery but were lethal for the infantry if they were held up, as they were so often by machine gun fire on 1 July.

In the Beaumont Hamel British Cemetery lies Pte. W. S. Lonsdale of the Lancashire Fusiliers. He was nineteen and from Salford, and his parents inscribed his tombstone: 'Our Loss, his eternal gain.' Close to him is Pte. F. A. W. Tagg, aged nineteen, a soldier of the Middlesex Regiment from Ealing: 'His memory is as dear today as in the hour he passed away.' Nearby is Pte. Frank Halliwell of the Lancashire Fusiliers, who was from Chorley and twenty years old when he died. 'He answered his country's call', wrote his family.

To the south of the 29th Division was the 36th (Ulster) Division, which managed, partly because they ran at the German trenches rather than walking, to break into the Schwaben Redoubt under the cover of smoke shells fired by trench mortars, having also crawled out into no man's land before Zero Hour. As early as 7.15 a.m., under cover of extraordinarily heavy fire—which the Germans described as the worst in the sector and which featured Stokes mortars and some 9-in. mortars firing 200 lb bombs lent by the French—the leading battalions of the 109th and 108th Brigades crept forward to within a hundred yards of the German front trenches. Recent battlefield archaeology shows that they dug into no man's land before the attack and therefore were so close to the enemy that they won the all-important race to the parapet. When the buglers in the front trench signaled 'Advance', the *Official History* records, 'the scene with the mist clearing off and the morning sun glistening on the long rows of bayonets was brilliant and striking'.[23] Back then, the anniversary of the Battle of the Boyne was celebrated on 1 July under the Old Style calendar, rather than on the 12th as it is today, and the Protestants among the Ulstermen believed the anniversary was a good augury.[*]

---

[*] Some Protestant officers wore the sashes of the Orange order into battle.

SCHWABEN REDOUBT
*British artillery bombarding the formidable German defence system
at the Schwaben Redoubt, 1 July 1916.*

On the right, the 109th Brigade managed to reach the German front trenches and to capture them with relatively few casualties, largely because the wire had been cut by artillery and trench mortar fire. It was on approaching the reserve trench 500 yards (457 m) beyond that the German machine guns doomed the advance, especially once the guns at Thiepval no longer had to be directed against the smashed 32nd Division. The 9th Royal Inniskilling Fusiliers took heavy losses, though by 8 a.m. they had entered the front face of the Schwaben Redoubt. Over four hundred prisoners were taken, to be escorted back to British lines at the rate of sixteen per guard. 'So anxious were they to reach shelter', stated one eyewitness, 'that many ran back towards the British lines, outpacing their escorts.'[24]

When the Ulstermen broke into the redoubt they found a huge rabbit warren complex* of tunnels, shelters, cavernous ammunition stores and dugouts built over the previous eighteen months, but they had to withdraw from it later that day when it became clear that the divisions on either side of them had not made their objectives and a massive counter-attack was on its way. The further the Ulstermen got the more exposed they became to counter-attack, especially once a heavy barrage cut them off from reinforcements. During the night and the next morning they therefore had to give up the positions they had fought so hard to gain. They won four VCs that day, and some units are thought to have penetrated up to 2 miles (3.2 km), but they lost 5,104 men, over one-third of the division.[25]

'The morning of July 1st broke very fine', wrote W. J. Grant of D Battery, 154th Brigade of the Royal Field Artillery in his diary,

> on a day which was to prove a red letter day for the division. As soon as day broke the infantry went over, with the 32nd Division on one side and the 29th Division on the other. Our infantry got away in fine style taking the enemy's first three lines in very quick time, it was in this line they were supposed to rest for half an hour, while the artillery shelled the fourth and fifth lines, but being carried away by the excitement they pushed on and took the 4th and 5th lines, in spite of the officers' pleading to them to rest. On getting into the front line they had Thiepval at their mercy, but it was discovered that neither of the 32nd or the 29th Divisions had got to the enemy's

---

* A section of the Mill Road Cemetery has gravestones that lie flat because the ground below them is so honeycombed that they would not stand upright.

first line, which of course left our division in a very sharp salient which was impossible to hold. We were being enfiladed from both flanks besides a murderous fire from the front. There was nothing to do but to draw back, which was very disheartening, seeing that the division had had 5,000 casualties in two hours getting there, but there was nothing else for it. By this time the battery had fired just on 4,000 rounds in just over a day.[26]

At noon a gun in Grant's battery took a direct hit from a German shell, 'severely wounding all four men. The gunpit caught fire, then fell in, burning and burying the gun.' Grant then watched the wounded from the 36th Division's attack returning:

> It was a terrible sight to see the wounded coming down in hundreds, the most serious in any convenience that was handy, in General Service wagons, motor-lorries, ambulances, or anything they could get. Those that could possibly crawl at all had to get from the trenches to the dressing station, which was about three miles (4.8km), as best they could... About 3 o'clock about 500 prisoners came down and looked pleased to be out of it. Night closed with the division cut to pieces, but still holding on to the enemy's second line.[27]

Grant survived through to demobilization in March 1919, but Rifleman W. Dunbar, nineteen, of the Royal Irish Rifles, from Downpatrick Street in Belfast, did not. He died of his wounds on 2 July and his grave is inscribed 'Peace perfect peace with loved ones far away'.

ROYAL IRISH RIFLES (OVERLEAF)
*Soldiers resting in a communication trench during
the opening hours of battle on 1 July.*

To the south of the 36th Division was the 32nd, which was supposed to take the Thiepval plateau high ground, a strong German position that would not fall for another twelve weeks. The division assembled on the lower slopes of the Thiepval spur from Authuille Wood to Thiepval Wood, where the assembly trenches had only been dug in the hard chalk a few days before, and the men had had to carry up supplies too, leaving them, in the words of one of them, 'dog-tired'.[28] The two front brigades, the 97th and 99th, had to attack the whole spur from the Liepzig Salient to Thiepval village, and then, it was hoped, advance further. The southern face of the salient was to be left alone and taken from behind once the other attacks had succeeded. It was a New Army battalion, the 17th Highland Light Infantry (Glasgow Commercials) of the 97th Brigade, which left their trenches at 7.23 a.m. and crawled to within 35 yards (32 m) of the German lines won the race to the parapet and took the Leipzig Redoubt, the only gain of the day for the 32nd Division.[29] Brig. J. B. Jardine of the 97th had learnt the tactic in the 1904–5 Russo-Japanese War where he had been a liaison officer with the Japanese, another example of a senior officer who was much more lion than donkey.

'The defenders were taken prisoner before they could emerge from their dugouts in the chalk quarry', recorded Edmonds.[30] Yet it was when the 97th Brigade tried to go beyond that, moving onto the trenches known as 'Hindenburg Strasse', across an open slope, that machine guns forced them to stop. From his observation post, Jardine ordered Lt.-Col. A. S. Cotton of the 161st Brigade of the Royal Field Artillery, which was supporting 97th Brigade, to switch part of his fire to the German defences at the rear of the Leipzig Redoubt, even though this was contrary to GHQ's orders. This allowed the Highlanders to withdraw successfully. 'It is the 32nd Division at its best', wrote an onlooker, Percy Crozier of the 36th Division:

> I see rows upon rows of British soldiers lying dead, dying or wounded, in no man's land. Here and there I see an officer urging on his followers. Occasionally I can see the hands thrown up and then a body flops to the ground. The bursting shells and smoke make visibility poor... Again I look southward from a different angle and perceive heaped up masses of British corpses suspended on the German wire in front of the Thiepval stronghold, while live men rush forward in orderly procession to swell the weight of numbers in the spider's web.[31]

The Lonsdale Battalion, part of 97th Brigade, moved to Crucifix Corner near Authuille Wood prior to the attack, in which their task was to assault the Leipzig Salient and capture the German advance HQ at Mouquet Ferme.* The men mainly hailed from Cumberland and Westmoreland. Their commanding officer, Lt.-Col. Percy Machell, was under no illusions about how hazardous it was going to be to carry out the complicated order to leave the wood at 8 a.m. and go northwards until they reached the rear of the right company of the HLI and then swing due east, all under what he rightly suspected would be heavy machine gun fire not just from the opposing German trenches but also enfilading fire from machine gun nests that

---

* The Lonsdales' official title was XI (Service) Battalion Border Regiment (Lonsdale).

doglegged to the right. 'If it goes badly,' he wrote in his final instructions, 'I shall come up and see it through.'[32]

'The Lonsdales wished each other luck and shook hands,' records their historian, 'then they started to advance, some cheering and singing as if at a football match.'[33] They moved in what was called 'blob formation', in small groups slightly to the rear and flank of the group in front, which was considered the best position to adopt under shellfire. Yet it was not shell-fire they had principally to worry about as a hailstorm of bullets 'cut furrows in the earth as the machine-gunners found their range'. Seeing what was happening, Col. Machell 'rushed to the front to lead his men on', whereupon he was immediately shot through the head, and his adjutant Lt. Gordon was severely wounded as he stood over the body. By then Maj. Diggle, the second-in-command, was already wounded. Pte. Thomas Hart-ness, from the village of Skelton in Cumbria, who had joined up aged only sixteen, was killed next to Machell, and watching him die was Richard Hartness, his nineteen-year-old brother, who was to die of wounds six weeks later.* The Lonsdales who survived the opening machine gun bursts, all too few of them, nonetheless pressed on, joined up with the HLI as planned and captured the German front trench, which together they man-aged to defend from counter-attack.

An account of going over the top was left by an unnamed nineteen-year-old member of B Company of the Lonsdales, which deserves repetition:

* There were another two brothers from Skelton, George and John Watt. Despite being shot through both thighs, George returned to fight with the Lons-dales. John Watt was killed at Passchendaele in November 1917.

What a long quarter of an hour it seemed to me. I wished
hundreds of times it was up, every minute seemed like
an hour. My heart thumped so hard I am sure it could be
heard, but others must have felt the same as nobody com-
mented on it. All talking stopped and to this day I can't
say for sure whether the order came to fix bayonets or not,
I was so worked up. The suspense ended with the command 'Come on "B" boys get out', or something like that.
I set my teeth and jumped out of the trench and followed
the rest in single file. Captain H was standing at the edge
of the trench the same old smile on his face and as cool as
if he was on parade.[34]

It did not last long. Within moments:

A machine gun somewhere opened out. A bullet burned
at the back of my neck. TN, my best pal dropped, I looked
back to see if he was wounded or what, he raised himself
up on his hand, gave a smile and then drooped back—he
gave a shudder and then lay still. I knew he was out. This
lad was only seventeen… We had barely gone another
5 yards [4.5 m] when it seemed to rain bullets, it was hell
let loose. The Corporal dropped, shot through the hand.
I made one dive for a shell hole for cover.* A few more
dropped beside me; we stayed there for a moment, we
had only got to our feet again when those cursed machine
guns opened up worse than ever.[35]

Although the young soldier did move closer to the German lines
in a small group, they were all killed save him: 'Men were laying
every few yards and some were hanging on the German wire.'

* Shell-holes could be enormous: at the Hunters Cemetery at Beaumont Hamel
an entire cemetery of the 51st Division is incorporated into a single one.

He stayed still in no man's land, while those who moved were killed by sniper or machine gun fire. 'A bumblebee buzzed once or twice round my head then settled on a flower,' he recalled, 'up above a skylark was singing.'[36] At one point 'A man jumped up screaming "Mother, Mother", he made towards me tearing at his clothes. I shut my eyes expecting to feel his hands at my throat but he ran past me towards the German trenches. The poor fellow must have went mad with pain or something.' Afterwards the narrator was wounded in the hand and elbow by shrapnel but got back safely to the British trenches and made his way to the dressing station. 'The whole place both inside and out was crowded with wounded, some seriously, others, like myself with nice cushy ones. Dead men were laid out all round, some covered but the majority as they had been carried in.'[37] Of Col. Machell, he wrote that he 'died like the man he was, and the way he would have wished, leading his beloved battalion in one last rush against almost impregnable positions.'[38]

'Throughout that long blazing summer's day,' writes the Lonsdales' historian, 'shocked men, their uniforms torn and bloodied, clung to shell holes out in no man's land as shells fell among them, praying for night.'[39] Of the 28 Lonsdale officers and 1,800 men who left Authuille Wood that morning, 23 officers and 500 men failed to attend evening roll-call. Back in the villages and towns around Penrith there was hardly a house which did not have its blinds drawn once the post offices there and in Appleby, Shap and Tebay started to deliver the hundreds of much-feared telegrams, and newspapers published the photographs of local men under the headline: 'Fallen for their King and Country'.[40]

FIRST CASUALTIES
*Wounded British soldiers resting
at Mametz, July 1916.*

To the south of the 32nd Division was the 8th Division, whose duty it was to capture the Ovillers spur to the north of the Albert–Bapaume road, a very wide section of no man's land 750 yards (686 m) across. Maj.-Gen. Henry Hudson chose to attack with three brigades abreast of each other. Some 200 men of the 2nd Middlesex and 2nd Devonshires captured the German second-line trench, a number that was down to only seventy by the time they were forced to retreat at 9.15 a.m., but on their left the 70th Brigade made it to even the third line of trenches.[41] As so often elsewhere, however, the German barrage managed to cut these men off from reinforcements, a situation that the General Staff did not seem to have reckoned with, or at least for which they had no answer. The 2nd Middlesex suffered 540 casualties that day, and two months later its commander, Lt.-Col. E. T.

Falkner Sandys DSO, shot himself in the Cavendish Hotel in London while convalescing from his five wounds. 'I have never had a moment's peace since July 1st', he said in his suicide note. Overall the division suffered over five thousand casualties, while only managing to inflict 280 on the Germans.

The battleplan of the 34th Division to the south of the 8th was to attack over a frontage of 2,000 yards (1,829 m) towards La Boisselle with the 102nd Brigade on the left and the 101st on the right. They were intended to take the German front and intermediate lines, before the 103rd Brigade passed through them to capture the day's ultimate objective, the village of Contalmaison. As it was, La Boisselle did not fall for another two days and Contalmaison not until 10 July. Lt. (later Lt.-Col.) Walter Vignoles was company commander of D Company in the 10th Battalion Lincolnshire Regiment (Grimsby Chums)* and recorded how 'There was a kind of suppressed excitement running through all the men as the time for the advance came nearer.'42 Pte. Harry Baumber recalled how at 6 a.m. that morning he and a dozen friends 'had a bit of a sing-song in one of the dug-outs. I remember two of the songs very well—"When You Wore a Tulip" and "I Love the Ladies".'43†

Vignoles and Baumber were so close to the La Boisselle mine when it exploded at 7.28 a.m. that the chalk came down around them in the form of powder, making it hard for them to see anything. 'We seemed to be very close to it and looked in awe as

* The only Pals battalion to be called Chums.
† Of that dozen, only Baumber and his comrade Sam Ward were able to answer roll-call that night.

great pieces of earth as big as coal wagons were blasted skywards to hurtle and roll and then start to scream back all around us', wrote Baumber. 'A great geyser of chalk, mud and flame had risen and subsided before our gaze… I vividly recall as the barrage lifted and there was the very slightest pause in this torment, several skylarks were singing.'[44] It did not last long, for as Baumber wrote:

> By now it was over the top and away down a gentle slope to the German lines behind a line of steadfast men walking grimly forward and wondering what was in store. We soon found out. I noticed men falling thick and fast about me and all the time a remorseless chatter of machine guns. It was akin to riding into a hailstorm… All too soon it was obvious Jerry had not been obliterated, his wire was not destroyed and we had been called on to walk 800 yards [732 m] across no man's land into Hell. A far cry from the walkover we had been promised… We who were left were simply pinned down where we lay. There was no going forward and at this time no way of getting back to our lines—an absolute bloody and desolate shambles. If you moved an inch it brought a sweeping crackle of fire and we survivors began to realise our only hope was to wait until dark, but that was a long way off. We also realised, lying there in shell holes, that the Grimsby Chums must be no more.[45]

He was right; of the full complement of officers who were with the battalion when it was formed, only three were left. In their first ever attack, the Chums had achieved nothing, at the cost of 502 casualties, of whom 187 had been killed. With a fighting strength of 849, some 59 per cent of those who took part in the assault were listed as dead, wounded or missing by the end of the day. When Baumber returned to Grimsby in February 1917 he described it as 'a town in mourning after the Somme with almost every street affected in some way'.[46]

The Tyneside Scottish and Tyneside Irish battalions also suffered terribly that day, for equally little gain. 'As the time approached, I passed the word along for the men to get their hats on and for the pipes to get going',[47] recalled Capt. Herries of the Tyneside Scottish. 'The pluckiest thing I ever saw was a piper of the Tyneside Scottish playing his company over the parapet in the attack on the German trenches near Albert', recalled an unnamed officer of the 2nd Middlesex Regiment.

> As their officers gave the signal to advance I saw the piper—I think he was the Pipe Major—jump out of the trenches and march straight over no man's land towards the German lines. The tremendous rattle of machine gun and rifle fire, which the enemy at once opened up on us, completely drowned the sound of his pipes. But it was obvious he was playing as though he would burst the bag, and just faintly through the din we heard the mighty shout his comrades gave as they swarmed after him. How he escaped death I can't understand for the ground was literally ploughed up by the hail of bullets. But he seemed to bear a charmed life and the last glimpse I had of him, as we too dashed out, showed him still marching erect, play-ing furiously, and quite regardless of the flying bullets and the men dropping all around him.[48]

It was Pipe Maj. John Wilson and he won the MM, the cita-tion reading, 'For conspicuous bravery and devotion to duty on 1 July 1916'.

PIPE MAJOR
JOHN WILSON
*The Tyneside
Scottish soldier won
a Military Medal for
indefatigably playing
his pipes through-
out his company's
advance towards the
German lines.*

Someone else for whom the pipes were drowned out by the ordnance was Pte. J. Elliot of the 20th Battalion, who said: 'I never heard the pipes but did see poor "Aggy" Fyfe.* He was riddled with bullets, writhing and screaming. Another lad was just kneeling, his head thrown right back. Bullets were just slapping into him knocking great bloody chunks off his body.'[49] Piper Alexander Boyd of the 22nd Battalion wrote to his mother

* LCpl. Pipe Garnet Wolseley Fyfe was Pipe Maj. Wilson's uncle.

from a hospital in Cambridge after having a finger shot off: 'The only thing disabled is the pipes, I got them blown away when I was playing the charge... I was playing "Tipperary" and all the boys were singing and shouting. I could see them falling all about me. It was a lucky day for me that I was not blown away. I shall never forget it as long as I live.'[50]

Although only 120 seconds had passed between the blowing of the mines at 7.28 a.m. and the launch of the attack, the Bavarian machine-gunners were already in place as the Tyneside Scottish advanced towards them at walking pace. They allowed the Tynesiders to get to a midpoint across no man's land before unleashing their retribution. 'You know Fritzie had let us come on just enough so that we were exposed coming down that slope,' recalled Pte. Elliot. 'That way we would cop it if we came forward and cop it just as bad if we tried to go back. We were just scythed down.'[51] The German machine-gunners were ordered to fire at the thighs, so that there would be a good chance of a second bullet hitting as their victims fell. 'It was hell on earth,' recalled Pte. William Bloomfield of the same battalion, 'that is the only name I can give it. We were the first over the trenches after the sign to advance and never a man faltered. It was like going to a picnic, the way the men marched on, but it was only for a few yards, until the Hun got sight of us.'[52]

The 20th and 23rd Battalions Northumberland Fusiliers (Tyneside Scottish) were caught in devastatingly accurate cross-fire from Hptm. von Rohr's 55th Bavarian Landwehr Regiment from the directions of Ovillers and La Boisselle. 'We swarmed over the parapets at a given time and we went over the ground as if on parade, but it was a tough job', Pte. Thomas Grant of the

23rd Battalion wrote to his wife. 'Numerous German machine guns thinned the Scottish ranks, but still the men went forward. It was glorious!'

A few of the men reached the German second line of trenches, but all too few, and those who did were all but wiped out. The 4th Tyneside Scottish lost the third highest number of men of any battalion that day. Because the men were given strict orders not to stop to look after the wounded in order to maintain their forward momentum, there were heart-rending scenes on the battlefield. 'That was awful, hearing men who were your mates pleading with you and pulling at your ankles for help but not being able to do anything', recalled a soldier of the 20th Battalion. 'One lad alongside me was chanting "Mother of God No! Mother of God No!" just like that. Others were effing and blinding. I don't know how I got through it. I could see men dropping all around then [his sergeant] Billy [Grant] yelled "Down on your bellies!"'[53]

Although they threw themselves down, they were now effectively pinned down in no man's land somewhere between the Tara–Usna Ridge and La Boisselle, and as another survivor later wrote:

> Pzzing, pzzing, those machine gun bullets came buzz-
> ing through the grass all around us. Through the din we
> could hears screams behind us but no one dared look
> round. It would have been suicide just to raise yourself up
> to look. At one moment there was silence—maybe Fritzie
> boy was changing his ammunition belts. At any rate for
> a few moments above it all we could hear was larks. A
> bomber near me shouted 'Hey, I've been shot in the arse!'
> Billy Grant shouted back, 'Haven't we all!'[54]

There were plenty of examples of extraordinary bravery that day. As an unknown Tyneside Scottish corporal reported to the *Evening Chronicle*: 'One of our chaps did an amazingly plucky thing. He was a bit of a sprinter and easily outdistanced the rest of us, so he dashed right up to a machine gun that was worrying us and put it out of action on his own.'[55] It was all too rare an occurrence, however, especially with the heavy packs that so many of the men were carrying. Capt. Herries reached the second line of German trenches, but 'Beyond that they were very strong and several of us who got over the parapet had a hot time of it'. Pte. Tommy Easton of the 21st Battalion found that the wire 'was reasonably destroyed and we tumbled into the first German trench we came to'. But as an unnamed corporal also recalled, 'The Huns fought desperately and we had a tough job of clearing them out. They simply crushed us with machine gun fire. It was real red blistering hell hot and make no mistake.'[56]

Because 101st Brigade was slightly slower to move off at Zero Hour, the 21st Battalion of the Tyneside Scottish suffered heavier casualties. 'I don't know how I got through it,' recalled Pte. J. Barron. 'I could see men dropping all around, and then someone yelled "Get down! Get down!" and I was on my belly for the next eleven hours. I crawled, if you stood up the machine gun would get you for sure.'[57] The brigade bombing company assaulting La Boisselle beckoned the 21st up to support them, but the machine guns prevented it. 'The lads up in front must have put up a good fight', recalled Pte. Elliot, 'because we could hear bombs and shouting and Lewis guns well into the afternoon. So if the lads in front went down, they went down fighting.'[58] The Germans, well dug in at La Boisselle and largely unaffected by the barrage, were able to man their positions before the British bombers of the 21st and 22nd Battalions Tyneside Scottish could arrive, a story that was repeated up and down the entire northern and central sectors of the line.

Capts. W. Herries and J. M. Charlton managed to get a Lewis gun up into a hollow in the ground outside La Boisselle and, in Herries' words, 'Then we gave it to them hot', but 'Further along Forster, McIntosh and Lamb got over with a party of men, but the whole lot were mown down by a machine gun'. Back in their hollow, as Herries wrote, 'For a while we did great execution but the gun jammed at a critical moment. Poor Charlton was shot down while attempting to charge a German strongpoint and the initiative passed to the enemy.'[59] Herries defended the lines that had been captured as best he could, but reported how exhausted his men were, and how he 'had to pull myself together with a mouthful of brandy once or twice'. In all, the 34th Division suffered 6,380 casualties for next to nothing achieved.[60]

In Ovillers British Cemetery lies Lt.-Col. F.C. Heneker, aged forty-three, who commanded the 21st Battalion Northumberland Fusiliers (Tyneside Scottish) and whose gravestone reads: 'He died the noblest death a man may die.'

To the south of the 34th was the 21st Division, which needed to break through north of Fricourt. It took 4,256 casualties in the unsuccessful attempt, some of which were entirely unnecessary, as when A Company of the 7th Green Howards attacked a German machine gun team at 7.45 p.m. on its own and without orders, in what has accurately been described as 'one of the most bizarre episodes of the whole battle'.[61] The company was under orders to hold the front-line trench until 2.30 p.m. when they were to join an attack with other troops, but the very experienced Maj. Kent saw the damage being done by a machine gun and presumably thought he could take it out with a determined rush. Personal initiative always carries a risk and he was among the one hundred fallen. The machine gun was still in action in the afternoon when it cut down another battalion.

Pte. Daniel Sweeney of the Lincolnshire Regiment was a Regular soldier who had joined the army in 1907. He was discharged in March 1919, by which time he had married when on leave. He had four sons, all of whom were to serve in the Second

PRIVATE
DANIEL SWEENEY
*A soldier of the
Lincolnshire Regiment,
he fought for three
days and two nights
without relief during
the first days of
the Somme.*

World War. In a letter home simply dated July, he wrote, 'I must tell you what I know and saw of this murder; I think I am allowed to tell you and it will be a truer story than what you have read in the papers, at least I think so.'[62] In their support role, the 1st Lincolns had to 'get across the German trench with our loads as quickly as possible... but as soon as were all on top the Germans started sending big shrapnel shells—terrible things—I heard when we got into the German first line of trenches... we lost twenty-four men killed by one shell.' That night they had to relieve the men in front of them:

> We were in the firing line all night of the 1st, all of the 2nd and were relieved on the night of the 3rd by the [redacted by the censor]... When I think of my poor dear chums who have fallen I could cry. I have had to cry about one of my chums who has been out here since the beginning of the war and had not received a scratch, poor lad he died game with his mother's name his last word. You cannot realize what it is like to see poor lads lying about with terrible wounds and not being able to help them. We came out of action with 4 officers out of 26 and 435 men out of 1,150. I am glad to say that most of them are wounded, not killed, and I can say that for one of our dead there are ten German dead. I have accounted for fourteen I am certain of but I believe I killed twelve in one dugout. I gave them eight bombs, one for Kitchener and the others for my chums.[63]

To the south of the 21st Division was the 50th Brigade of the 17th Division, which had been ordered to capture Fricourt but also utterly failed to reach its objective. The future military journalist and historian Lt. Basil Liddell Hart observed how the German 110th and 111th Reserve Regiments' fire 'was so deadly that our men were forced to crawl... Our battalion lost about 500 men crossing 180 yards [165 m] of no-man's land'.[64] The experience was to affect his view of military tactics for the rest of his life, making him deeply sceptical of the direct frontal assault and a passionate theorist of the war of manoeuvre.

Gunner Gambling spent 1 July in front of Fricourt Wood too. As he wrote at the time:

> The morning of the eighth day [of the bombardment, i.e. 1 July] found a steady fire proceeding from our guns, and it also revealed great devastation in the enemy's lines. At 7.30 a.m. (the time for which thousands of men had been waiting anxiously, and which had arrived at last) the Infantry (prepared for the great work in hand) were ready to leave the trenches at the given signal. At last the signal was given, and the officers leapt on to the parapet of the trenches, then raising their arms above their heads, gave a lusty shout to the men to follow. In a second the men were over the top and rushing towards no-man's land shouting and singing at the top of their voices, hundreds of them falling, never to rise again. The rest still rushing on to enter the Germans' first-line trench, and then to forge further on into the enemy's support trenches where they were met with a fierce shower of machine gun bullets, which were soon overcame... The infantry did wonderful work on that morning (the wonderful 1st of July) and in less time than it takes to tell had cleared the enemy right back and the cavalry were standing by ready to take a hand.[65]

'Reports up to 8 a.m. most satisfactory', wrote Haig in his diary that day. 'Our troops had everywhere crossed the Enemy's front trenches.'[66] He was still being given deeply over-optimistic estimates, as only five of the seventeen British divisions achieved that key objective.[67]

There seem to have been two very different battles being fought on 1 July, the ones north and south of Fricourt. The great difference between them was that German guns were destroyed in large numbers in the valleys north of Mametz and Montauban, such as those of the German 12th Division which lost most of its guns.[68] The British were also greatly helped by the fact that, having 386 aircraft to the Germans' 129, the aerial observers were able to correct the Allied fire against the Germans. 'The numerical superiority of the enemy's airmen,' wrote General von Arnim, 'and the fact that their machines were better made, became disagreeably apparent to us, particularly in their direction of the enemy's fire and in bomb-dropping.'[69]

The 7th Division to the south of 50th Brigade had the duty of capturing Mametz, south-east of Fricourt, which they managed to achieve by 4 p.m.[70] 'Very noisy night, fine morning', noted Maj. Probert who was serving with the 7th Division's artillery.

> Started our final intense bombardment at 6.25 a.m., lifted at 7.30 a.m. Milne went forward as FOO [forward observation officer] but was hit by shrapnel in our own front line... From the Observation Point we could see the infantry with the pink squares of flannel on the packs and bayonets flashing in the sun climbing up the hill towards [the] Fritz trench. They appeared to have the front line two supports without too much difficulty but the snipers had now come up from the deep dugouts and were causing a lot of casualties and were trying to bomb us out of Mametz Trench... One captain [of the] Gordons was

sitting in the front line eating his lunch with one hand
and shooting the snipers with the other as they came
out to surrender. I thought that rather rough as some
had their hands up but he said that he had had several
wounded Jocks shot on their stretchers.* There were a
great many dead lying about, both Gordons and Boche.
Whilst we were waiting to get on, the 2nd Warwicks
made their second attack across the old no man's land
shouting their war cry 'Warwicks' to clear the old Boche
front line and support of snipers: the first troops having
moved on without mopping up... This was a very noisy,
alarming and bloody affair. The cries of the wounded for
stretcher-bearers who couldn't be attended to because
of snipers were distressing. Although the Boche trenches
were flattened by our bombardment the deep dugouts
were hardly affected and spewed out snipers who
effectively prevented movement until this second attack
(Warwicks) was made.[71]

Afterwards Probert remarked: 'White Trench [in front of
Bazentin-le-Petit church and Bazentin-le-Grand Wood] was
only half dug and I could see our chaps almost from the waist
up as they moved down the trench from Beetle Alley throwing
an occasional Mills bomb, the sharp 'ping' accompanied by a
cloud of chalk dust... Col. Longbourne said that the Huns were
so scared by the shelling from our 4.5 How[itzer]s that some of
them had shat their pants.'[72]

Buried in the Dantzig Alley British Cemetery is Lt. Warwick
Hall, twenty, of the South Staffordshire Regiment, the twin

---

* Today 98 men of the 2nd Battalion Gordon Highlanders are buried in a small
circular cemetery on the side of the Péronne–Albert road.

THE 'LUCKY' WOUNDED
These men have 'Blighties' that invalided them out of
the trenches and back home, at least temporarily.

son of Walter and Frances Hall of Hodnet, Shropshire, who has 'Thy will be done' for a headstone. Mary Louise White of Bournemouth, the mother of Capt. J. V. White, twenty-four, of the Manchester Regiment, wrote on his grave marker: 'I thank my God for all my remembrance of thee. Mother.' A second lieutenant, J. H. Parr-Dudley, twenty, of the Royal Fusiliers, who came from East Malling in Kent and whose brother was also killed during the battle, lies beneath a quotation from the poet Rupert Brooke:

I found you white and radiant
Sleeping quietly,
Far out through the tides of darkness[73]

Those who remained of the 8th and 9th Battalions of the Devonshires later that same day buried their fallen comrades in the same trench from which they had gone over the top. They erected a wooden memorial in Mansell Copse with the words: 'The Devonshires held this trench. The Devonshires hold it still.'

Maj.-Gen. Ivor Maxse's 18th (Eastern) Division made the deepest territorial gains of the day, partly due to the training regime imposed by him on this New Army unit.[74] Although it was the division's first battle it behaved like an elite force, and by 3 p.m. had captured all its objectives, albeit at a cost of 3,115 men. There was a good deal of hand-to-hand fighting; the 7th Buffs were given the task of clearing the old mine warfare Carnoy craters of men of the 6th Bavarian Regiment, for example, which took ninety minutes of brutal, exhausting bayonet fighting. 'Dead British and Boche, in couples, were found afterwards, each man transfixed by the other's bayonet', recalled an eyewitness.[75] The diminutive but fierce Sgt. P. G. Upton killed ten men in this crater-fighting.*

Seeing the danger of a British breakthrough, the German High Command gave orders for all available men—including clerks, cooks, batmen and 200 raw recruits—to occupy the second position to prevent it falling. The 109th Reserve Regiment had lost 42 officers and 2,105 other ranks, while the 6th Bavarian

---

* He was later to die of wounds received at the battle of Poelcappelle in 1917.

Reserve Regiment had lost 35 officers and 1,775 men.[76] Yet the British High Command did not move the 9th (Scottish) Division forward to take advantage of this momentary opportunity.

There were plenty of stories of devotion to duty in the division, such as that of LCpl. G. Bilson, a runner, who was sent off to the 55th Brigade HQ with the historic message that the East Surreys had captured their final objective at 12.30 p.m.

MAJOR–GENERAL
IVOR MAXSE
Maxse, pictured here presenting medals to men of the 152nd Highland Brigade, made the greatest territorial gains of the 1 July commanding the 18th Division.

The corporal did not return till the next morning. 'I noticed', said Col. Irwin of the East Surreys later, 'that his clothes and equipment were in tatters, and that his eyes were crossed in an extraordinary way. "Where have you been," I asked. He said he had delivered the message, and coming back was blown up. He had only come to himself half an hour before but his first thought, you see, was to report himself.'[77]

The most southerly division in the British army on 1 July, the 30th Division under Maj.-Gen. James 'Jimmy' Shea, was charged with taking the village of Montauban, which it achieved by 1 p.m., though with the loss of 3,011 men.[78] The division was enormously aided by the way that the British and especially the French artillery had managed to destroy deep German dug-outs in and around Montauban. 'They looked monstrous, lying there crumpled, amidst a foul litter of clothes, stick bombs, old boots and bottles', the journalist Philip Gibbs wrote of the German corpses there. 'Others might have been old or young. One could not tell because they had no faces and were just masses of raw flesh in uniforms.'[79]

In the attack on the southern sector at Montauban, Lt.-Col. Bryan Fairfax, who commanded the 17th Battalion King's Liverpool Regiment, and Commandant Le Petit of the 3rd Battalion of the French 153rd Regiment left the trenches and crossed no mans land arm-in-arm, in a display of Allied unity. 'This battalion moved forward,' reported Le Petit's colonel, 'as practised during manoeuvres, and managed to sweep its way over five lines of enemy trenches covering an 800 metre (875 yd) stretch. German prisoners and weaponry were taken.' Although Fairfax was gassed near Guillemont on 29 July, he survived the war, as did Le Petit, who was appointed to the General Staff.

When the 18th Manchesters went into the attack, Pte. Ted Higson recalled the way those men from the Liverpool and Bedford who had been wounded earlier,

> were shouting out to us 'Good luck Manchesters' as suddenly we began to notice the enemy artillery fire increasing, shells began to come over thick and fast. We were also being swept by machine gun fire from the left. Our fellows were falling right and left... impossible to hear orders, but we looked to our captain. He was holding up his hand for a halt; our hearts were filled with anxious fears that we had failed. But no—we were only waiting until the unit on our left, which had been held up by barbed wire, got over the obstacle and cleared away the Germans who were hammering us on that side. We waited twenty minutes and then started again, all the time our wounded comrades were calling out for help and begging for drinks.[80]

They left them for the RAMC to deal with later. 'When we reached within a hundred yards of the village [of Montauban], our artillery barrage lifted as we unslung our rifles and charged the waiting Germans', Higson continued. 'They fired at us until we got up quite close to them and then the row of steel got to make for them and scrambling out of their trenches they ran for it. Many of them did not run far, for the aim of our boys was splendid.'[81] They captured Montauban Alley on the far side of the village. That night Higson slept until the enemy's artillery opened up on their position at dawn on 2 July, and after a German counter-attack they were relieved by the Wiltshires.

To the south of 30th Division, straddling both sides of the river Somme, was the French 6th Army under Gen. Fayolle (part of Foch's Army Group). Its experience was summed up in one page of the *Official History*, accurately entitled 'The Complete Success of the French on 1st July'.[82] South of the Somme the French had built up a ten-to-one advantage in heavy artillery, 84 batteries to the Germans' eight. North of the Somme, next to the British 30th Division, was the French XX Corps under Gen. Balfourier. In that sector a German officer claimed to have 'counted as many as two hundred explosions a minute', and in the final forty-eight hours before the attack his men had received no food as a result of the bombardment, and, 'At each explosion, the earth shook over a wide area.'[83] Next to XX Corps was Gen. Berdoulat's I Colonial Corps and then Gen. Jacquot's XXXV Corps, with Gen. Duchêne's II Corps in reserve.

Maurice Balfourier's XX Corps attacked with two front-line divisions at 7.30 a.m., which were helped by a thick morning mist on the Somme that allowed them to reach the German trenches largely unseen. Although there was severe hand-to-hand fighting in Bois Favière, whose north-eastern corner was retained by the Germans for several days, otherwise Gen. Nourrisson's 39th Division (next to the British 30th Division) took all his objectives so quickly that at noon he proposed attacking Hardecourt in front of him, but could not do so because the British XIII Corps had not yet reached its second phase positions.[84] He did, however, use rifle fire to repulse no fewer than four German counter-attacks from Hardecourt.[85]

Gen. Vuillemot's 11th Division meanwhile captured the Y Wood Salient at the first assault, but failed to capture Curlu on its right flank until the evening. So by the end of 1 July XX Corps had captured the entire German first position with few losses and no use of its own reserves. The French corps south of the river did not attack until 9.30 a.m., so they were able to take the enemy by surprise. Although the village of Frise was held by the Germans, the Colonial Corps took the villages of Dompierre and Becquincourt. By noon it had captured all its initial objectives and was pushing on towards Herbecourt and Assevillers, and by nightfall the corps had taken 2,000 prisoners and was ready to attack the Germans' second position the next day.* The XXXV Corps attracted the fire of the German divisions further south, but nonetheless it too was very successful, and altogether the 6th Army achieved all its objectives and took 4,000 prisoners.[86]

Rawlinson was not ready to take advantage of this break-through, however, but kept his cavalry reserves north of the Albert–Bapaume road all day and failed to deploy his infantry reserve, the 9th (Scottish) Division. Haig, who unlike Rawlinson at least did believe in the possibilities of a breakthrough, was impressed by the successes in the south—even sending a telegram to his wife boasting of them at 10.55 a.m.—but he too failed to take advantage of the success there.†

---

* The French Serre-Hébuterne Nécropole Nationale has several Algerians and Moroccans buried in it, noticeable from the domed headstones denoting Muslims instead of the Christian cross.

† The very fact that he had time to contact Lady Haig on the first day of the Somme Offensive rather underlines Churchill's criticism in his biography of the Duke of Marlborough of 'our latter-day generals' that 'There are no physical disturbances: there is no danger: there is no hurry...There is nearly always leisure for a conference even in the gravest crisis.'

The first day of the Somme Offensive ended with the British army having captured less than 3 sq. miles (7.7 sq. km).[87] Before 9 a.m., Lady Haig later claimed, 'satisfactory progress was made... Douglas was very pleased with the early success of the morning.'[88] Yet that was because he was misinformed of what was happening. Of his war diary reports that the 31st Division 'was moving into Serre village', for example, he later wrote, 'This was afterwards proved to be incorrect'. Another report that 'our troops... were entering Thiepval village' he later qualified with the words 'This did not prove to be the case.' Later on in the same diary entry he wrote: 'On a 16-mile [26 km] front of attack varying fortune must be expected! It is difficult to summarise all that was reported. After lunch I motored to Querrieu and saw Sir H. Rawlinson. We hold the Montauban–Mametz Spur and villages of those names... our men are in the Schwaben Redoubt... the Enemy counter-attacked here but were driven back... I am inclined to believe from further reports that few of the VIII Corps left their trenches!'[89] This monstrous slur—the Newfoundlanders were in the VIII Corps, as were several other units crucified before Beaumont Hamel—along with the imputation he made against the 137th Brigade of the 46th Division serves to illustrate how bad was the 'fog of war' that day.

'Haig has been demonized in popular memory as the chief butcher and bungler', the historian Brian Bond has written, 'among a generation of callous and incompetent generals responsible for mass slaughter in a futile conflict.'[90] Although Bond rightly deplores this, it must be said that Haig left plenty of evidence in his own handwriting to support the unfair thesis.

In 1936, in a memoir entitled *The Man I Knew,* Haig's widow wrote that on 1 July 1916: 'Our troops crossed the [German] frontline trenches everywhere on a front of 16 miles [26 km].'[91] Only five of the seventeen divisions that attacked achieved anything like this. In some cases they could not even cross the *British* front-line trenches, but were massacred in the attempt.

On 4 July Lieutenant-General Hunter-Weston, who commanded VIII Corps, which incorporated 4th, 29th and 31st Divisions, wrote to the men of VIII Corps to say:

> All observers agree in stating that the various waves of men issued from their trenches and moved forward at the appointed time in perfect order, undismayed by the heavy artillery fire and deadly machine gun fire. There were no cowards or waverers, and not a man fell out. It was a magnificent display of disciplined courage worthy of the best traditions of the British race... We had the most difficult part of the line to attack... By your splendid attack you held the enemy forces here in the North, and so enabled our friends in the South, both British and French, to achieve the brilliant success that they have. Therefore though we did not do all that we hoped to, you have more than pulled your weight... We have got to stick it out, and go on hammering. Next time we attack, if it please God, we will not only pull our weight, but will pull off a big thing... I rejoice to have the privilege of commanding such a band of heroes as the VIII Corps have proved themselves to be.[92]

As an exercise in putting the best face on the disaster, it was not bad, but VIII Corps was never again given responsibility for participating in a major or minor British offensive for the rest of the war, and was broken up in the summer of 1918.[93] Hunter-Weston himself was not allowed to conduct another major attack for the duration, although he found time to get elected as Unionist MP for North Ayrshire only five months after the Somme.[94]

SIX

AFTERMATH

By hedge and dyke the leaves /
Flame to the clay / Fanned by the wing /
Of Death. Yet Life achieves / From such decay /
The buds of spring. / By air and sea and earth /
To glorious death / Our loves we gave /
Certain that Death is Birth /
Love blossometh / Beyond the grave.[1]

CAPT. CHARLES K. MCKERROW,
'Flanders', October 1915

*

'We worked for three days
and three nights without rest. It was
the bloodiest battle I ever saw.'[2]

PTE. H. STREETS,
58th Field Ambulance

'THE NEWFOUNDLANDERS HAD BEEN WIPED OUT AT Hamel and the South Wales Borderers at Beaumont', wrote John Harris in *Covenant with Death*. 'The Durhams had been decimated at Ovillers and the Green Howards at Fricourt. Whole battalions, thousands on thousands on thousands of men, had been swept away in an unbelievable butchery in the first five or ten minutes after seven-thirty.'[3] Almost half of the 120,000 men in the 143 battalions who had gone over the top on 1 July 1916 had become casualties, a truly staggering toll in warfare ancient or modern.[4] Of the total of 57,471 casualties, 993 officers and 18,247 other ranks were killed, 1,337 officers and 34,156 other ranks were wounded, 96 officers and 2,056 other ranks were missing and 12 officers and 573 other ranks were prisoners of war.[5] The total figures were therefore 35,494 wounded, 19,240 killed, 2,152 missing and 585 POWs.[6]

No fewer than thirty-two battalions suffered more than five hundred casualties each, out of a typical full complement of around 1,050. The 10th West Yorkshires, which lost a staggering total of 710, headed this doleful list, followed by the 1st Newfoundland, which lost 684, the 4th Tyneside Scottish (629), 1st Tyneside Irish (620), 8th Yorks and Lancs (597), County Down Volunteers (595), Donegal and Fermanagh Volunteers (589) and 1/8th Royal Warwicks (588). Eighteen of the thirty-two lost twenty or more officers and none lost fewer than a dozen, out of a normal complement of thirty, making the pro rata officer casualty rate slightly higher than that for the other ranks. While one battalion of the thirty-two was from the empire (the New-foundlanders), four came from the Territorial force and seven from the Regular army. No fewer than twenty of the battalions taking the greatest losses were from the New Army, the 'Pals' who had answered Lord Kitchener's call.[7]

Sometimes it can be hard to visualize such huge numbers. To get a sense of the extent of the slaughter, roughly the same number of Britons (and Newfoundlanders) were killed and wounded on the first day of the Somme as there are words in the main body of text in this book. It is impossible to accommodate this size of loss, however, though Lady Haig tried to in her memoirs. 'The total casualties for the first three days' fighting were about 40,000. Douglas was at first much concerned by the seemingly high figure, but he discovered that it included a great many lightly wounded cases which in other armies would not have been evacuated at all. Well over 4,000 prisoners were captured during the first phase of the attack.'[8] (In fact the number of POWs was somewhere between 2,000 and 2,500.)[9]

The number of soldiers of the BEF killed on 1 July 1916 was almost as great as the 21,000 who died in the three years of the Crimean War or the 21,000 who died in the three years of the Boer War. As an extreme example, the Charge of the Light Brigade—remembered as an iconic disaster for British arms—cost 110 dead, whereas the first day of the Somme killed 175 times that number. Around 3 per cent of Britain's casualties for the First World War were suffered on that one day alone, although it was not the worst one-day loss of the war; on 22 August 1914 the French lost 27,000 killed in 'the Battle of the Frontiers' in Alsace-Lorraine.[10]

NEWFOUNDLAND MEMORIAL
*The unveiling of the memorial—a proud caribou—to the Newfoundland
dead at Beaumont Hamel, 7 June 1925.*

'It was pure bloody murder', recalled Pte. P. Smith of the 1st
Border Regiment of the first day on the Somme. 'Douglas Haig
should have been hung, drawn and quartered for what he did
on the Somme. The cream of British manhood was shattered in
less than six hours.'[11] The pioneer battalions attached to each
division, which had been intended to repair the captured German trenches, were set to work burying the dead. 'For this disastrous loss of the finest manhood of the United Kingdom and
Ireland there was only a small gain of ground to show,' recorded
the *Official History*,

although certainly the greatest yet showed by the British Expeditionary Force: an advance into the enemy's position some 3½ miles [5.6 km] wide and averaging a mile in depth… Of the magnificent successes achieved by the 30th, 18th, 36th (Ulster), 4th and 56th Divisions, none except those gained by the two first on the extreme right, next to the equally successful French, were permanent. The others were no more than isolated thrusts which, in the absence of support on either side, could not be maintained.[12]

'The officers went through the same as the men,' Pte. Thomas Grant of the 23rd Battalion Northumberland Fusiliers (Tyneside Scottish) wrote to his wife, 'they knew no fear.'[13] Of course they did indeed know fear, but they also knew that leadership meant not communicating it to their men. Nor was it only the more junior officers who were killed, the lieutenants, captains and majors; a total of forty-seven brigadiers and lieutenant-colonels were casualties leading from the front on that first day, the majority of them killed.[14]

French casualties amounted to 7,000, German losses between 10,000 and 12,000.[15] At the cemetery which houses the German dead from the whole offensive, the Deutscher Soldatenhof at Fricourt, there are 11,970 bodies buried in four large ossuaries, of which 6,477 are unknown. A total of 17,027 are buried there, including those soldiers killed in battles from July to November 1916.* The Royal British Legion and the local French communities lay wreaths there every year.

* In 1940 the Nazis desecrated the graves of Jews who died fighting for Germany; these have since been replaced and many have several small stones on top of them indicating visits by mourners.

THE PRIDE OF ULSTER
*A memorial to the Ulster dead in Sydenham,
east Belfast, unveiled in 2010.*

The Thiepval Memorial to the Missing is a hugely impressive 46-metre (150 ft) high brick and stone structure, designed by Sir Edwin Lutyens, that bears the names of over 72,000 soldiers of the United Kingdom and South Africa* who died on the Somme and who have no known grave. Many bodies had to be left on the battlefield, and those that were hastily buried in the front lines often lost their improvised markers when that

* Other Commonwealth countries have their own memorials to the missing, at Villers-Bretonneux, Vimy and elsewhere.

sector came under renewed bombardment, so that 'the ceaseless pounding of the artillery meant that many of the bodies simply vanished'.[16] Others were blown to smithereens by the shelling, and so could not be identified.

During the Somme Offensive, more newspapers than ever before published the full casualty lists, including provincial papers. They also published letters from the front that openly discussed the conditions in the trenches. One of the first—and certainly the best known—official war films, *The Battle of the Somme*, was released in August 1916 and played in over two thousand British cinemas. It was silent, in black-and-white, seventy-five minutes long, and some 20 million people watched it in the first six weeks after its release.[17] It had been seen by over half the country by the time the battle ended in November.[18] Some of its scenes had to be cut for reasons of national morale and the only action sequence in it was probably staged—including its most famous moment, in which a group of soldiers clamber out of a trench only for one of them to be shot and fall back into it—but at least it was honest about the high casualties.[19] Scenes include the explosion of a mine, wounded soldiers returning to their lines, an artillery barrage and destroyed buildings, yet neither the film nor the casualty lists led to an outbreak of pacifism amongst the public, which, fortunately for Britain, was not to manifest itself until the war had been safely won. 'In this picture the world will obtain some idea of what it costs in human suffering to put down the Devil's dominion', wrote one newspaper review.[20] Its realism was commended by the *Manchester Guardian* and *The Times*. Frances Stevenson, secretary and mistress of David Lloyd George (then Minister of Munitions in

'THEIR NAME LIVETH FOR EVERMORE'
One of the beautifully kept cemeteries along the Serre Road where many unknown British soldiers, who fell on 1 July, are buried.

prime minister Herbert Asquith's cabinet), whose brother had died on the Western Front, wrote in her diary: 'I have often tried to imagine myself what he went through, but now I *know* and I shall never forget.'[21]

We tend to focus today on the 'headline' figure of the number killed on the first day of the Somme, but almost twice that number were wounded, many very seriously.[*] The medical services were of course prepared for large numbers of wounded over the course of the whole offensive, but not for anything like so many on its first day. In general, the doctors, surgeons, nurses, orderlies, ambulance drivers and stretcher-bearers who had arrived to

[*] The emergency medical kits the men were given were not intended for bad wounds, merely consisting of a cotton dressing and a small bottle of iodine.

serve the wounded of the First World War in 1914 were unprepared for what awaited them on the battlefields of the Western Front. Not only were the numbers of wounded higher than predicted, but also the types of wounds suffered were very different from what had been expected.[22] The days of neat holes being made by rounded bullets were gone, to be replaced by horrific injuries caused by shrapnel and serrated shell fragments, and poison gas destroyed lungs.

By the time of the Somme Offensive, after the tragedies of 1914 and 1915, Regimental Medical Officers (RMOs) had a much better idea of what to expect, but as the latest historian of the wounded of the First World War points out, 'Carefully planned entraining and detraining routines went to pieces in the face of the sheer numbers of casualties at the railheads, and within a week of the Somme the whole system of transit simply broke down.'[23] Nurse Morgan of the RAMC, for example, only realized the true extent of the problem when the No.3 Ambulance Train on which she lived and worked pulled into a base station to deliver its load and found 2,000 men from an earlier train still lying on stretchers on the platform, the sidings and in rooms in the station. There was no room to take her patients off the train, and would not be for hours until the previous train's arrivals could be moved. Even though she did her best to calm her patients, 'all around them they could hear the moaning of men in agony'.[24] It was a scene that was being replayed behind the whole front, and got much worse later in the battle when temporary ambulance trains—ordinary trains pressed into service for the emergency but not properly kitted out for their new use and only intended for the lightly injured—had to be used to transport all types of wounded. Stretchers were laid end-to-end in the corridors, and were hung from every strap.

Medical officers were appallingly overworked. Charles McKerrow had been an Ayrshire GP before volunteering as an RMO for the Northumberland Fusiliers, a regiment that lost 2,440 men killed and wounded in the first few hours of its attack on La Boisselle.* When McKerrow's 10th Battalion went into action a week later and captured a German aid post, he took it over, complete with its German casualties and a German medical orderly who insisted on helping him. They treated 1,000 casualties as the piles of blood-stained bandages were trampled into the mud.[25] 'No one could have possibly equalled my stretcher-bearers,' he wrote to his wife after working continually for ten days, living off coffee and soup but with virtually no sleep. 'As one hard-bitten chap said to me, "they are doing Christ's work". It really is very fine to see these chaps passing through storms of shell to help their comrades. I am very proud of them and hope they will get some rewards apart from the normal ones of their conscience.'[26] He later ensured that three of them were decorated.

Not everyone was sad to be wounded, so long as it was the right type of wound. When considering how he survived the battle years later, Pte. Bert Payne of the 8th Manchesters said: 'I suppose it was having the wound, a "Blighty", to get away from the Somme. Everyone wanted a Blighty but it depended on what kind it would be, a good one or a bad one, and mine was a bad one.'[27] After lying fully conscious in no man's land

* Seventy of whom came from one small mining village alone.

for seven hours after being shot in the mouth by a machine gun bullet in the attack on Montauban, Payne and his comrade Bill Brock, who had lost a foot and used a rifle as a crutch, slowly and immensely painfully made their way back to the British lines. In a shell-hole on their way, Payne used Brock's rifle to shoot a British soldier who had been 'almost blown to pieces, but somehow [was] still alive. He was gasping for air, sobbing and calling out for someone called Annie.' Payne later said he 'could see at a glance that there was no hope for the man: he was bound to die after hours of lonely agony.'[28] It is very likely that a lot more of these mercy killings took place in no man's land than survivors cared to remember or admit, and they should be seen as rugged acts of charity.

When Payne and Brock finally made it back to the British lines, which they found in chaos, there was a horse-drawn ambulance preparing to leave, full of wounded Germans. In an equally ruthless act of kindness for a comrade, Payne 'tipped enough men off their stretchers to make space for his wounded friend, leaving them on the roadside calling for help'. He later found another ambulance cart for himself, and as it bumped along towards the medical station at Abbeville he 'watched walking wounded and carts full of dead moving in one direction and reinforcements rushing' towards Montauban.[29]

On the second day of the offensive, 2 July, in the north of the battlefield around Gommecourt, Serre and Beaumont Hamel, a number of short and uncoordinated armistices were brokered as the Germans permitted the British to retrieve their wounded.[30] This was nothing like the de facto Christmas Truce of 1914, but it was an indication perhaps that all civilized behaviour had not been entirely eradicated. 'In many places,' wrote an historian, 'when they realized their own lives were no longer at risk, [the Germans] ceased firing, so that the more lightly wounded could make their way back as best they could do their own front line.'[31]

Some of the badly wounded did not get back until 4 July, and many others not at all. Gerald Brennan, a young officer who captured ground at the end of July, noticed how soldiers wounded on 1 July had often 'crawled into shell-holes, wrapped their waterproof sheets round them, taken out their bibles and died like that'.[32]

Opposite Serre, where German snipers had been shooting at British wounded caught on the barbed wire, Harry Siepmann,

TOMMY TRIUMPHANT
*A Tommy of the Royal Fusiliers from Maxse's 18th Division, sporting
a particularly fine pickelhaube at the capture of Theipval, 26 September 1916.*

an Old Rugbeian artillery officer fresh out of Oxford, saw an extraordinary sight from his forward observation post. Two men climbed out of the British trench, without a white flag, where-upon 'a stretcher was passed to them, and they proceeded to carry it through no man's land. Hundreds, perhaps thousands, of eyes must have been upon them, and all firing of any sort ceased. Complete, uncanny silence descended like a pall, as the two men trudged steadily on and stopped beside a body lying on the ground. They lifted it onto a stretcher and plodded slowly back the way they had come. The silence remained unbroken until they were safe, and then the war resumed.'[33] Some chivalry in war still existed, although in places where both sides went out to collect casualties simultaneously there was virtually no frater-nization. Nonetheless, at Gommecourt the Germans raised a Red Cross flag early on 2 July for a one-hour truce in which their 2nd Reserve Guards Division did help British stretcher-bearers bring in the wounded.[34]

A truce that had been expressly forbidden by GHQ went ahead at Beaumont Hamel anyway on 2 July, though from the German side there might have been a self-interested aspect to it, besides mere human decency. Lt.-Col. John Hall, who commanded the 16th Battalion Middlesex Regiment, and who had been wounded in the attack, recalled how at 2.30 p.m. the Germans raised a white flag 'and sent over stretcher bearers to no man's land; in addition to helping our wounded, he was no doubt helping himself to the machine guns, Lewis guns, rifles, etc., lying about close to his front line.'[35] When this was reported to the brigade HQ, further permission to send out stretcher-bearers was refused, and orders issued to fire on the German

A DEAD CAPTAIN
*A German grave for an Allied soldier
at Gommecourt.*

stretcher-bearers. 'These instructions were not acted on with
any enthusiasm by our riflemen in the front line', recalled Hall.
This was understandable; it offended the norms of civilized
behaviour that still mattered to the British Tommy, would not
redound well on the captured British POWs and would dis-
courage future truces of that nature, but above all it would sen-
tence to death any men still trapped in shell-holes between the
lines. Sure enough, as Hall recalled, 'Thereafter, whilst daylight
lasted the enemy was reported as firing on any wounded man in
no man's land who showed the slightest movement.'[36]

'We started to retrace our steps to the assembly trench, back
over the battlefield of yesterday, now strewn with thousands of

our boys and the enemy', wrote Ted Higson of the Manchester Pals on 2 July. 'It was awful to see the boys who forty-eight hours ago were full of life, now lying on the battlefield... The Sergeant-Major was there calling out the names—some were answered, others would never hear their names again on this earth but by this time would be answering the roll call on the other side... From July 2nd to 8th we were occupied in re-organizing ourselves and burying the dead. The latter was worse than all the fighting, a nightmare to us all.'[37] On 9 July Higson was wounded in the shoulder by shrapnel and he was sent back to England.*

Soon after 1 July, Gen. Maxse visited the 11th Royal Fusiliers, which had done very well near Montauban, to congratulate them. 'Morning gentlemen, damn good show, thank you very much, you did very well, marvellous', he told Lt. Richard Hawkins and his fellow officers. 'Tell me, where would you expect to find a group of officers congregated together in the middle of the greatest battle there has ever been?' He answered his own question: 'I'll tell you, walking about on the skyline looking for souvenirs! I saw them through my field glasses.'[38] (Hawkins himself had managed to pick up a magnificent pickel-haube helmet.) The robbing of both friendly and enemy corpses is understandably not an aspect of the war mentioned in the official histories, but it was certainly widespread on both sides. An aspect of this practice was that anything valueless found in wallets, such as personal letters, were discarded. As Pte. Stephen Graham of the Scots Guards recalled of this paper debris on

* Later, he was awarded a commission and in 1917 he returned to France to command a platoon.

the Somme battlefield, 'When the wind rose they blew about like dead leaves. There were photographs, too, prints of wife and sweetheart, of mother, or perchance a baby born whilst the father was at the war—priceless, worthless possessions.' Graham watched a gunner from a 60 lb battery searching the corpse of a German machine-gunner 'without success, and he gave the dead body a kick. "The dirty bastard," said he, as if he were accusing the corpse. "Somebody's bin 'ere before me."'[39]

On 3 July the writer Robert Graves, who served with the Royal Welch Fusiliers, went into Mametz Wood looking for German overcoats to use for himself and his men at night. In his haunting autobiography *Goodbye to All That*, he recorded how,

> It was full of dead Prussian Guards Reserve, big men,
> and dead Royal Welch and South Wales Borderers, little
> men. Not a single tree in the wood remained unbroken.
> I collected my overcoats and came away as quickly as I
> could, climbing through the wreckage of green branches.
> Going and coming by the only possible route, I passed
> by the bloated and stinking corpse of a German with his
> back propped against a tree. He had a green face, spec-
> tacles, close-shaven hair; black blood was dripping from
> his nose and beard. I came across two other unforgettable
> corpses: a man from the South Wales Borderers and one
> of the Lehr Regiment had succeeded in bayoneting each
> other simultaneously.

Later in the battle Graves was wounded by a shell fragment through the lung and was wrongly reported to have died from his wounds.*

---

* He of course went on to write *I, Claudius* (1934), amongst much else.

Sir Douglas Haig started his diary entry for 2 July 1916 with the words: 'A day of downs and ups!'[40] With the enemy holding Fricourt, La Boisselle and Thiepval, and two battalions cut off at both the Schwaben Redoubt and at Serre, he was characteristically positive as he and Launcelot Kiggell went to church that morning and then motored over to Querrieu to see Rawlinson, whom they ordered to capture Fricourt 'and then advance on the enemy's second line'.[41] The fog of war was rarely foggier. Haig added in his diary that the adjutant-general, Lt.-Gen. George Fowke, had reported to him 'that the total casualties are estimated at over 40,000 to date. This cannot be considered severe in view of the numbers engaged, and the length of front attacked.'[42] In a letter to his wife on 3 July, Haig wrote: 'Things are going quite satisfactorily for us here, and the Enemy seems hard pushed to find any reserves at all.' This sense of quasi-success was surprisingly widespread after the greatest single-day disaster ever to overcome British arms; Gunner Gambling recorded how at 11.20 a.m. on 2 July 'we received the news that the German losses were greater than our own'.[43] It was completely untrue, of course, but good for morale.

It was not until 6 July, almost a week afterwards, that the High Command knew for certain the sheer scale of the catastrophe in terms of killed, wounded, missing and captured.[44] Before that Haig and his Staff did not fully understand that the attack had failed north of the Albert–Bapaume road, despite some expensive successes at the Schwaben and Leipzig Redoubts, and that this failure was not compensated for by XV and XIII Corps' limited successes south of the road, or even the success of the French. Of course the offensive could not be simply broken off because of the terrible losses on the first day. 'Day One on the Somme', points out one historian, 'was Day 132 at Verdun.'[45] And the attack had been co-ordinated with more than just the French; the Russians were also simultaneously attacking on the Eastern Front and the Italians on the Isonzo River, so the Somme Offensive was part of the war's first—and as it turned out, last—fully co-ordinated, simultaneous attack by all the Entente Powers. The continued attack on the Somme did indeed put huge pressure on the Central Powers, as both Hindenburg and Ludendorff were later to acknowledge, with the latter stating that the battle meant that Germany 'had to face the danger that "Somme fighting" would soon break out at various points on our fronts, and that even our troops would not be able to withstand such attacks indefinitely'.[46]

So the British kept up the mutually murderous assaults for five more months, with Sir William Robertson, the Chief of the Imperial General Staff, telling Haig from London on 7 July: 'We have these Germans this time… if we take the chances offered.'[47] After the disaster in the northern sector became apparent, Haig and Rawlinson concentrated on the southern sector, and in the first half of July the British 4th Army and French 6th Army continued their attacks, pushing the Germans back towards Bapaume at terrible cost. Strategically speaking it bore fruit: from 2 July onwards, the Germans started withdrawing heavy batteries from the Verdun attack and transferring them to the Somme for defence. Nine days later, on 11 July, Gen. von Falkenhayn ordered the German army to go onto 'the strict defensive. The serious crisis in the Somme battle did not permit of the continuation of the attacks against Verdun.'[48]

It was Lt.-Gen. Walter Congreve[*] who came up with the idea of an innovative dawn surprise attack by his XIII Corps on 14 July.[49] This succeeded in capturing the German second-line position, and Haig hailed that day as 'the best day we have had in this war'. Yet it was not the much needed breakthrough, and by 24 July he was describing his strategy as being to 'peg away slowly eastwards'.[50] By the end of July the drive had fizzled out, despite a Reserve Army attack on Pozières Ridge. By then X Corps, which had been shattered at Thiepval, had been removed from the front line to 4th Army reserve. It was only given minor roles in the 1917 battles and stayed in rear areas in 1918 until its commander, Lt.-Gen. Sir Thomas Morland was removed from command that April.[51]

In all, the British suffered 82,000 further casualties between 5 July and 14 September on the Somme, although of the 141 days of the battle the first was by far the worst in terms of casualties.[52] Despite worsening weather and catastrophically mounting casualties, the 4th and Reserve (later 5th) Armies continued attacking the German positions until 18 November 1916.

In early August, Prince Rupprecht of Bavaria reported to Hindenburg: 'Though on a front of about 28 kilometers [17 miles] they have driven a wedge of about 4 kilometers [2.5 miles] depth, they themselves will not assert, after their experiences of July 20th, 22nd, 24th and 30th that the German line has been shaken at any point... The total losses of our enemies must amount to about 350,000, while ours, though regrettable, cannot be compared to theirs so far as numbers are concerned.'[53]

---

* Congreve was a true front-line general, 'absolutely indefatigable at getting to see for himself', even though it cost him his hand in 1917.

GERMAN PRISONERS OF WAR
A clearing depot in Abbeville,
northern France.

Tanks were first used on 15 September 1916 at Flers and Courcelette, and then put into action again ten days later. They succeeded in taking much of the original German third line, but by that time the enemy had built a fourth and fifth line of defence in front of Bapaume, the original final target on 1 July.[54]*A soldier called Bert Chaney recorded what it was like when the thirty-six Mark 1 tanks, each weighing 30 tons (29.5 tonnes) and with a top speed of 8 kmph (5 mph), were unleashed: 'We heard strange throbbing noises, and lumbering slowly towards us came three huge mechanical monsters such as we have never seen before. My first impression was that they looked ready to topple on their noses, but their tails and the two little wheels at the back held them down and kept them level.' Chaney, a 19-year-old signals officer with the Territorial 7th London Battalion, recalled how the tanks 'moved on, frightening the Jerries out of their wits and making them scuttle like frightened rabbits.'

That same day, 15 September, the prime minister's son, Lt. Raymond Asquith, was killed, and a future prime minister, Capt. Harold Macmillan of the 4th Battalion Grenadier Guards, was badly wounded. Macmillan lay throughout the morning and early afternoon in a shell-hole in no man's land, where he first read Aeschylus' *Prometheus Bound* and then took morphia, before his company sergeant-major found him, saying, 'Thank you, sir, for leave to carry you away.' A future cabinet colleague of Macmillan's, Capt. (later FM) Harold Alexander of the 2nd Battalion Irish Guards, also fought that day; of his battalion of

---

* At Amiens in 1918, tanks were to halt one of Hindenburg's major offensives, and later that year they broke through German lines, also at Amiens.

1,000 only 166 men were still alive and uninjured by the end of it.[55] On 14 November, just as the battle was ending, the writer Hector Munro—whose sublime short stories were published under the pseudonym 'Saki'—shouted 'Put that bloody cigarette out!' to a comrade, but it was too late; a German sniper had seen the light and fired, killing Munro, whose body was subsequently so badly ground into the mud that it was never found. His name is on the Thiepval Memorial.

'Our losses in territory may be seen on the map with a microscope', wrote Prince Rupprecht of Bavaria on 15 September.

> Their losses in that far more precious thing—human
> life—are simply prodigious. Amply and in full coin have
> they paid for every foot of ground we sold them. They
> can have all they want at the same price... We are not,
> like the Entente generals, forced to throw raw, untrained
> recruits into the very front of the fighting... It saddens
> us to exact the dreadful toll of suffering and death that is
> being marked up on the ledger of history, but if the enemy
> is still minded to possess a few more hectares of blood-
> sodden soil, I fear they must pay a bitter price.[56]

Yet by then he was wrong; the Germans had begun to lose more men than the British, even taking into account the losses on the first day of the offensive.

It was not until the end of September that the British captured Thiepval and at no point during the entire battle did the British get further than 7 or 8 miles (11.3 or 12.8 km) from their original 1 July positions. By then it was very much an imperial battle, involving Australians, Canadians, New Zealanders, South Africans and Indians, as well as of course as the remaining Newfoundlanders.[57]

On Sunday, 15 October, 2nd-Lt. Alfred Pollard of the 1st Battalion Honourable Artillery Company, a London insurance clerk who was later to win the VC, was scouting out in no man's land in the cold and damp under a full moon, his face blackened with burnt cork and revolver in hand. 'I had not proceeded very far before I felt something yield and scrunch under me', he recalled in his autobiography. 'It was the skeleton of a corpse, its bones picked clean by the army of rats which scavenged the battlefields. The rags of a tunic still covered its nakedness… Further on I found another; then another and another. They were the bodies of those slain in the fighting at the beginning of July. All were British.'[58]

The Battle of the Somme ended on 18 November 1916, having cost the British army 419,655 casualties, an average of almost 3,000 per day.[59] In all, the 141-day battle between 1 July and 18 November 1916 left 1.22 million men dead or wounded, of whom 194,451 were French.[60] The German figure was around 600,000, but it is very hard to tell accurately as they only took count of their wounded every ten days whereas the British did so every single day. So a German soldier might have been wounded, patched up and returned to his unit within ten days and it would not show up in the figures whereas it would have in the British statistics.

Over the whole Somme Offensive, over four and a half months, the maximum depth of advance was 8 miles (12.8 km) of devastated ground, six villages and some woodland, along a 20-mile (32 km) front.[61] From Albert to Berlin there was still another 585 miles (942 km).

THE ALLIED CEMETERY AT FRICOURT
This cemetery contains graves where more than one casualty is buried
and on which more than one headstone is erected.

Morale remained surprisingly high in the British army then and afterwards, despite the losses of the first day. In 1917 French units refused to return to the front line and their commander, Robert Nivelle, was relieved of his post. The French mutinies of 1917 were not against the war, argues one historian, 'but against the murderous way in which it was being fought'.[62] Nivelle's replacement, Philippe Pétain, restored order partly by shooting about forty mutineers (out of half a million), initiating reforms and halting frontal assaults.* By contrast, morale in Haig's

---

* The forty men received posthumous pardons in the 1930s on the basis that they had been denied the right of appeal. In 1998 the then prime minister Lionel Jospin stated that they were 'restored to their full place in our national collective memory'. The same has not happened to the 343 Britons shot for cowardice and other reasons in that war.

British army was far better than in the mutinous French and Russian armies in 1917 or the equally mutinous German and Austrian armies the following year.

The Battle of the Somme changed the war psychology of both Britain and Germany, broadening the boundaries of what nation-states felt able to inflict upon each other. After it, the Germans moved to unrestricted submarine attacks in the Atlantic, recognizing that since they probably could not defeat the British in a conventional land or sea battle they must try to starve Britain into surrender.[63] When this unrestrained assault saw American commercial ships also sunk, it had the effect of bringing the United States into the war on the Allied side, with huge strategic implications. Furthermore, there could be no peace after the Battle of the Somme, except after total victory; so many men could not be seen to have died for a patched-up semi-peace.

'Neither Haig's view of Lloyd George nor Lloyd George's view of Haig is likely to be accepted by history', wrote Winston Churchill in *Great Contemporaries*. 'They will both be deemed better men than they deemed each other.'[64] The Somme left Lloyd George 'deeply shaken', as the size of the losses were unprecedented in British military history, although they were proportionately the same as those suffered by the Germans and certainly the French at Verdun, or the Union and Confederates armies at Antietam.[65] 'The horror of what I have seen has burnt into my soul,' he told his mistress Frances Stevenson on his return from visiting a friend's partially paralyzed son in hospital, 'and has almost unnerved me for my work.'[66] The battle left Lloyd George preferring a strategy of peripheral attacks, despite Robertson and Haig insisting that the Germans could only be defeated on the Western Front. Unable to sack Haig for political reasons, after the Somme Lloyd George instead undermined him, and by 1918 hoped to have him superseded by Pétain in the Supreme War Council.

The Battle of the Somme also brought a new degree of respect for the British army in Germany. The British-born Princess Evelyn von Blücher (née Stapleton-Bretherton), noted how much it had 'veered round' attitudes in Berlin. 'Men who were scoffing and railing at England twelve months ago are beginning

HAIG'S FUNERAL
*Earl Haig's funeral on 3 February 1928 saw
huge crowds lining the streets of London.*

to express their admiration, and even dare to display a certain affection and attachment publicly.'[67] In February and March 1917 the Germans, by then suffering from a severe manpower crisis, abandoned their positions on the Somme and went back to their pre-prepared ones on the Hindenburg Line 20 miles (32 km) behind the Somme front. This retreat was presented in the press as 'an elastic bend' in the front line, but soldiers were returning home with harrowing stories of the sheer firepower of the British artillery. The Battle of the Somme saw the pendulum of war swing in the Entente's favour for the first time, though of course not on its first day. The Germans had retained the initiative, an all-important factor in warfare, throughout 1914 and 1915, and to an extent during the Battle of Verdun. It was at the Somme that the British and French wrested it from them for the first time, and although it was to be lost for short periods afterwards—primarily during the Ludendorff Offensive in the spring of 1918*—the Allies retained the power of initiating the action for the rest of the war.

The Battle of the Somme also brought to leadership in Germany the two warlords who were to guide its fortunes for the rest of the war, and became as powerful as any dictators: FM Paul von Hindenburg as Chief of the Great General Staff, and his chief executive officer Gen. Erich Ludendorff. The latter was appointed on 20 August 1916, as the battle was unfolding, and he immediately set about building the immensely powerful and easily defensible Hindenburg Line. 'The more important

---

* When the Germans retook the Somme battlefields in a matter of hours—territory that it had taken them years to lose, with so much blood expended on both sides.

repercussions of the Somme were longer term,' in the words of one historian; 'ultimately it prompted Hindenburg's and Ludendorff's decision to step up armaments production, intensify Germany's submarine campaign, and shorten their lines in the west.'[68]

Haig claimed that the Somme had relieved Verdun, fixed the German army in place, and worn it down. His first point was true: yet it did not fix the German army so successfully that they were not able to reinforce the Russian and Rumanian fronts as the battle progressed.[69] Nor was the German army's morale broken for another two years.* Even when its confidence did eventually break, its members were still capable of occasional unnecessary viciousness. LCpl. George Lawrence Price, of the 28th Battalion Canadian Expeditionary Force, was shot dead by a German sniper at 10.58 a.m. on 11 November 1918, two minutes before the Armistice came into effect.

---

* In the last 12 days of September 1918 the BEF captured more Germans than during the entire five-month-long Somme campaign.

SEVEN

LESSONS LEARNED

'There is more to be learnt from ill-success—
which is, after all, the true experience—
than from victories, which are often attributable
less to the excellence of the victor's plans
than to the weakness or mistakes
of his opponent.'[1]

Preface to EDMONDS,
Official History of the Great War,

*

'The Battle of the Somme... marked the end of
the first and mildest part of the war; thereafter it was
like embarking on a different one altogether.'[2]

ERNST JÜNGER,
Storm of Steel, 1920

O N 9 JULY 1916 LT.-GEN. SIR AYLMER HUNTER-WESTON wrote to FM Sir William Robertson, the Chief of the Imperial General Staff. This was largely an exercise in covering his own back, since he had spoken to Robertson earlier the same day by telephone, but the reasons for the failure of the attack by his VIII Corps just over a week earlier were worth reiterating. 'We were mistaken in supposing that two battalions had got through to Serre', he wrote,

> and had been cut off by the Germans getting up out
> of the dugouts behind them. Later and more accurate
> information established the fact that these battalions, and
> the majority of the other battalions all along the front,
> were defeated by the enemy's artillery barrage, and by his
> machine gun fire, which in many cases simply wiped out
> the battalions before they reached the German trenches.
> The gallantry, discipline and devotion of our troops was
> beyond praise. But we had not knocked the German
> trenches about nearly enough to block their dugouts and fill
> up their trenches in the way the German artillery does to
> our trenches, and so... the German Infantry and machine-
> gunners were able to come out of their dugouts, and man
> their parapets, as soon as our men showed, and were thus
> able to prevent our men reaching their trenches. The
> reason for the lack of success... is that the Germans here
> had better trenches, and a much more powerful artillery.[*]

---

[*] Hunter-Weston was totally wrong about the Germans having a more power-ful artillery, it was simply much better concentrated. In fact VII and VIII Corps hugely out-gunned the Germans.

It was at Gommecourt, Serre and Beaumont Hamel that
they most feared attack. A contributory cause was the
inadequacy of the artillery and of the ammunition available… Of ammunition we had only about one and one-
third heavy howitzer shells per yard run of trench fire,
whereas we should have had ten per yard run. However,
this latter reason is for your ear alone, it is inadvisable to
give currency to such unpleasant and dangerous facts.[3]

If there is any consolation for the horrors of 1 July 1916, it is
that the BEF swiftly faced up to such 'unpleasant and dangerous facts' and embarked on a profound revolution in tactics at
many levels, in what has been correctly described as 'a steep and
agonizing learning curve'.[4] The ultimate result of this was to
create an army that by 1918 deserved to win the war. Of course
the lessons ought to have been learnt even before the war had
started: in the Boer War British troops had tried and humiliat-
ingly failed to cross what one historian has called 'a "fire swept
zone" dominated by the German-manufactured quick firing,
long range rifles and field artillery'.[5] Yet even if the lessons
of that war should have been learned without the massacre of
1 July 1916, they certainly were after it took place. Perhaps it
is part of the human condition to learn from defeat more than
from victory.

It is appropriate that 1 July 1916 fell on almost the middle
day of the middle year of the war, because it saw an entirely new
phase of the struggle on the Western Front, with industrialized
warfare the norm from then onwards. Eighty per cent of Britain's 2.7 million war casualties occurred after 1 July 1916.[6] Ten
days after the attack, Maj.-Gen. de Lisle also wrote a report

explaining why his 29th Division, which had numbered 11,797 men before the attack and had suffered 44 per cent casualties, had fared so badly. These included the strength of the German defensive positions, the lack of speed and surprise in the attack, the failure of the heavy artillery to demolish the German front line, the early explosion of the Hawthorn Ridge mine, and the poor performance of his sixteen Stokes mortars in their ten-minute bombardment.[7] Even if one ignores the largely irrelevant last reason—Stokes mortar fire was insignificant compared to the seven days of bombardment by the entire divisional field artillery—the others are devastating.*

British trench mortars were standardized after 1 July, with each infantry brigade operating a battery of Stokes mortars, while artillerymen operated medium and heavy mortars at the divisional level. It also now became common for brigades to group all their specialists into a bombing company of, typically, 120 men, who would operate in groups of thirty or so.

The best kind of bombardment to unleash was discussed by X Corps in 1917, which concluded that instead of a week-long preliminary bombardment of an entire region:

> The hurricane bombardment had the advantage of a more
> demoralizing effect probably and bringing the attack
> more of a surprise. On the other hand wire cutting was
> bound to be slow and deliberate and thus nullify attempts
> to surprise, though this could be discounted somewhat
> by having wire cutting down the whole British front, this
> still possibly concealing the point of attack. The long slow
> bombardment meant better and more careful observation

---

* After the war he criticized various army and corps commanders as well.

for effect, the possibility of daily aerial photographs to observe if the results were satisfactory and therefore promised to be more generally effective against the enemy's defences. In order to put an equal number of lead on the enemy's trenches during the short bombardment as compared with long, a larger number of guns would be necessary.[8]

On 1 July 1916 a lifting barrage had been used which simply moved on regardless of where the infantry was, which generally did not work; indeed the battle has been described as 'an awful demonstration of the penalties of poor infantry-artillery co-ordination'.[9] Yet by the attack of 15 September the concept of a creeping barrage, one that worked its way forward along with the attack in a scientific and co-ordinated way, had brought considerable success.

It started halfway across no man's land in case any Germans had crawled out there during the night, and then advanced at the rate of 100 yards (91 m) every four minutes, ahead of the infantry advance. Flash-spotting and sound-ranging and the development of a system of image analysis for the RFC photographs were useful in counter-battery fire.[10] After the first day on the Somme, the artillery also improved at the all-important counter-battery fire, and a new fuse for artillery shells made them much better for wire cutting. 'Eighteen pound shrapnel was not an ideal wire-cutter', wrote Maj. Probert years later. 'The 106 fuse HE would have been much more effective, but it was not yet available.'[11]

The British also became more imaginative in thinking up ways to use machine guns to kill Germans in the trenches opposite. 'We were especially irritated by one machine gunner', recalled Ernst Jünger, 'who sprayed his bullets at such an angle that they came down vertically, with acceleration produced by sheer gravity. There was absolutely no point in trying to duck behind walls.'[12] The British were developing the machine gun as an offensive weapon, a major step along the way to the important 'indirect machine gun barrage' that became a major feature of all British assaults from September 1916 onwards.

The triangles cut from biscuit tins which the men of the 29th Division had sewn on the back of their haversacks had been a disaster on 1 July. 'With the sun's rays shining,' records the historian of VIII Corps' attack, 'the plaque certainly showed up the position of the men lying on the ground, but as it was thought to have increased the casualties, it was never worn again.'[13]

Very importantly, in the weeks after the first day of the offensive, the men were ordered not to march line abreast but instead to make short rushes under covering fire in the manner of attack Haig had wanted originally but for which Rawlinson had thought the men under-trained.[14] As every battalion, division and corps was required to deliver a post-battle report with recommendations, leading to the publication of two new manuals which drew on the lessons learnt, infantry tactics improved. Examples of good practice were also circulated in the form of memoranda and notes, which also went towards the codification of battle drills in training pamphlets.[15]

On 1 July the main infantry formation around which the attack had been organised had been the company, yet by November it was the platoon of thirty or forty men, now transformed into four sections of highly interdependent and effective specialists, with an ideal strength per platoon of one officer and forty-eight other ranks. In February 1917 GHQ of the BEF published training pamphlets SS143, *Instructions for the Training of Platoons for Offensive Action* and SS144, *The Normal Formation for the Attack*.[16] The former opened by explaining that GHQ now considered the platoon the primary unit of assault. The issue of the two pamphlets together was necessitated, it said, 'partly by the shortness of time which is available for training, and partly by the lack of experience among subordinate commanders'. It stated that it was intended to be an aid to the platoon commander in training and fighting, not necessarily applicable in all situations, but a distillation of experience and knowledge. The 46th Division had meanwhile opened a school to teach the new techniques.[17]

Designed to cover both trench-to-trench attacks and fighting in the open, SS143 and SS144 covered most eventualities and were both of high quality; indeed, it has recently been pointed out that 'Any modern infantryman would recognise the principles expounded therein.'[18] It covered the important practicalities of laying wire, the construction of fieldworks, appreciation of ground, and the avoidance of points covered by enemy fire.[19] SS144 proposed a standard attack frontage for a battalion of just 200 yards (183 m), together with the recommendation of wide intervals between men, lines and waves of attacks, proving that the High Command now appreciated the value of highly dispersed 'attacks in depth'.[20]

Whereas in 1916 the loss of officers and NCOs had left the other ranks dispirited and leaderless, by 1917 a flood of training pamphlets had changed the system to ensure that every man in the attack knew precisely what was expected of him. Similarly, on 1 July there had been no concept of battlefield doctrine, as the different timings of the mines' explosions and the different methods of attacks employed by Jardine on the Leipzig Redoubt and the 36th (Ulster) Division on the Schwaben Redoubt all too clearly showed. Afterwards, a general doctrine began to be imposed, with positive results.

In terms of personnel, officers tended to be appointed much more on the basis of ability after 1 July, rather than on what they had done before the war broke out. Although only one divisional commander, Stuart-Wortley, had been dismissed, Lt.-Gen. Henry Horne was the only one of the corps commanders to be promoted during the rest of the war.

De Lisle's report had also stated that since surprise mattered and 'speed in crossing the area between our front trenches and the enemy's is essential, the leading troops should therefore be lightly equipped and should be trained to cross this zone in a rush.'[21] It helped if, as on 15 September, the attack took place at dawn rather than once the sun was up. By November the British were also using the underground trenches known as 'Russian saps' to dig closer to the enemy trenches, and rise up through the earth to attack, gaining the element of surprise. 'After the attack had failed the 29th Division started immediately to advance their trenches closer to the enemy', points out one historian.[22] The German use of snipers on the first day of the offensive confirmed the need for the skill of individual marksmen in the British army too; each company provided marksmen for a detachment of sniping specialists to be attached to battalion headquarters.

GERMAN SHARPSHOOTERS
Snipers were used to great effect by the Germans during the Somme;
here, a group of Germans on the river Aisne climb a tree
to pick off Allied soldiers.

On 9 April 1917 the British launched the Battle of the Scarpe at Arras and put into operation many of the lessons learnt on the Somme—and particularly from its disastrous first day. The integration of Lewis gun, rifle grenade and trench mortar fire with short rushes forward of riflemen and bombers, together with an increasing confidence in the gunners' ability to lay down effective creeping barrages, truly transformed the BEF's battlefield performance and, in the words of one historian, had turned the British army 'from a largely inexperienced mass army to a largely experienced one'.[23] Far from 'Kitchener's Mob', it was now the highly professional force that won the great victories of the last hundred days in 1918. 'The British army learnt its lesson the hard way during the middle part of the Somme battle,' stated Charles Carrington, an infantry officer, 'and, for the rest of the war, was the best army in the field.'[24]

We may recoil from the thought of generals learning by trial and error at the expense of hundreds of thousands of men's lives, but for all their many faults, Haig and his fellow generals were fighting a war that had no precedents in its awfulness and capacity for industrialized slaughter. Haig was a good diplomat in a Western coalition that would eventually include the French, Belgium, Dominion and American armies. He learned faster and better than any of the Allied generals how to defeat Britain's most formidable and efficient foreign enemy since the Battle of Waterloo. Although no one—not even his greatest champions—pretends that Douglas Haig was a Marlborough or Wellington, his recent biographer was right to dub him 'not... the greatest military figure Britain has ever produced, but... one of the most significant—and one of the most successful.'[25] Amongst military historians such as John Terraine, Brian Bond, Gary Sheffield and Hew Strachan, there has been a strong resurgence in Haig's favour, and they have largely restored his reputation, albeit not yet with the general public.

SIX MONTHS ON (OVERLEAF)
Men of the King's Royal Rifle Corps
after the first battle of the Scarpe at Arras in 1917,
where the British army put into practice many
of the lessons learnt on the Somme.

In the Battle of Amiens, which began at 4.20 a.m. on 8 August 1918, Haig and his General Staff put into operation everything they had learnt two years earlier, and to devastating effect. There was no long preliminary bombardment by an insufficiently large artillery force, but instead a short, massive, surprise bombardment. Instead of wide lines of men marching slowly across no man's land, 342 heavy tanks smashed through German lines, and 450,000 men in British Commonwealth and French divisions advanced behind a creeping barrage. Royal Air Force aeroplanes attacked the German lines, and cavalry regiments captured large numbers of prisoners of war. In that one day—which Ludendorff later described as 'the black day of the German Army in the history of the war'—Haig's force inflicted 27,000 casualties and broke through 4 miles (6.4 km) of German defences. 'I had no hope of finding a strategic expedient whereby to turn the situation to our advantage', Ludendorff later admitted.[26] In reply to his report to the Kaiser two days later, Wilhelm II wrote: 'The War must be brought to an end.' [27]

The sacrifice of 1 July 1916 had at last been justified.

CONCLUSION

'One's revulsion to the ghastly horrors
of war was submerged in the belief
that this war was to end all wars and Utopia
would arise. What an illusion!'[1]

CPL. J. H. TANSLEY,
9th Yorkshire and Lancashire Regiment

*

'As I was one of the lucky ones; I still say
I am glad I was there.'[2]

LCPL. C. F. T. TOWNSEND,
12th Middlesex Regiment

I̲t has been calculated that it would take three and a half days for the 888,246 British and Commonwealth troops who died in the First World War to march past the Cenotaph in Whitehall, London, even at four men abreast. Although the size of the losses in the entire 141-day Battle of the Somme were horrific on both sides, it was the Germans—with a much lower overall population than the Allies—who could least afford them. In terms of sheer attrition, therefore, the Allies 'won' the battle, even if the British suffered on the first day of the offensive what has rightly been described as 'the greatest tragedy of their military history'.[3] In the broadest sense, therefore, Capt. von Hentig of the German Guard Reserve Division was right when he said that 'The Somme was the muddy grave of the German field army.'[4]

In his (admittedly very self-serving) *War Memoirs*, David Lloyd George nonetheless described the First Battle of the Somme as 'this bull-headed fight' of 'horrible and futile carnage' and one of 'the most gigantic, tenacious, grim and futile fights ever waged in the history of war'.[5] His friend and erstwhile colleague Winston Churchill agreed. 'You know my views about the offensive so well that I do not need to set them out on paper', he wrote on 15 July 1916 to his brother Jack, who was on the Australian and New Zealand Army Corps staff, contrasting Haig's supposed stupidity with the men's courage. 'The marvellous devotion and heroism of the troops exceeds all that history records or fancy has dreamed', he wrote.[6] However much the revisionist and now post-revisionist battle has been fought over Haig's reputation, history has certainly agreed with Churchill about the troops' heroism.

'He does not appear to have had any original ideas', Churchill wrote elsewhere of Haig.

> No one can discern a spark of that mysterious, visionary, often sinister genius which has enabled the great captains of history to dominate the material factors, save slaughter, and confront their foe with the triumph of novel apparitions. He was, we are told, quite friendly to the tanks, but the manoeuvre of making them would have never have occurred to him... Here he stood at the head of an army corps, then of an army, and finally of a group of mighty armies. Hurl them on and keep slogging at it in the best possible way—that was war.[7]

Yet when Churchill himself tried to employ his own mysterious, visionary genius to break the charnel-house slaughter on the Western Front, it had led to the Dardanelles disaster.

Unlike the Dardanelles, there was no public inquiry into the carnage of 1 July 1916, indeed within six months Haig's chief of staff, Launcelot Kiggell, had been promoted to lieutenant-general and awarded a knighthood 'for distinguished services in the field'. Yet being chief of staff is a thankless task—the commander tends to get the credit for victory while the chief of staff gets the blame for defeat—and Kiggell was sacked by Lloyd George in 1918. Nor should there have been an inquiry—any more than there ought to have been over the Dardanelles either—because the British High Command did not callously send men to their deaths; there were logical and rational reasons for the assumptions they made, many of them based on the dreadful experience of the Battles of Loos and Neuve Chapelle. They were doing their best, but many of their assumptions were plainly wrong. The *Official History of the Great War* put 'the prime causes of the general failure' down to 'the strength and depth of the German position and its stout defence', adding that there was 'little hope of a decisive success until the morale of the German army was broken', which was not to happen until 1918.[8]

The other reasons for the failure given by the *Official History*—which was certainly no whitewashing text—were many and various, and deserve reiteration: 'No attempt was made to select for attack a part of the enemy front which had weak features: indeed the Somme sector might be said to be the strongest part. The date chosen was due to the condition of affairs at Verdun, not to the state of the preparations on the Somme... the late hour, and that in broad daylight, had been fixed and insisted upon by General Foch... and General Fayolle.'[9] Yet the primary reason for the failure to break through—that the artillery had far too many targets—was not highlighted.

'Was it a futile bloodbath dreamed up by criminally incompetent donkeys,' asked the historian Nigel Jones on the ninetieth anniversary of the battle, 'or a necessary battle of attrition that decisively weakened the German enemy and saved Britain's embattled French ally from collapse, albeit at the cost of so many lions?'[10] It certainly did save France from disaster at Verdun, which was a necessary prerequisite for ultimate victory, in a war that did have to be won. For the First World War was not futile; it was fought against a German Reich and its Austro-Hungarian ally that sought to dominate the European continent, and there was no quick or easy way to win a war against the two empires except with massive loss of life. It could not be done cheaply, any more than it could be won cheaply against the Third Reich a quarter of a century later, when the Russians lost 27 million killed, nearly half of them military.

Slaughter on the Somme was tragically unavoidable. The Allies were forced to try to liberate Belgium and northern France from the Germans in a war that could not have been fought in any other way than a series of attritional battles on a continental scale. That is the dreadful, inexorable truth, as is the fact that the British army needed to adopt far better tactics, and part of that steep learning curve had to evolve through trial and costly error. Nonetheless, Haig and Rawlinson had clearly adopted a hopelessly optimistic and unimaginative battleplan; which one of them was ultimately responsible for it is of interest to military historians but hardly anyone else.

The extension of the bombardment for two extra days because of the rain reduced the stockpile for the final shelling, though it is doubtful that it could have been much more intense than it was. Yet despite the 1,627,824 shells fired, the front was so wide and deep that they simply were not enough, so that 'many strongpoints and machine gun posts were never touched'.[11] Not enough gas shells were fired, only a 'negligible quantity' by 75-mm gun batteries that had to be lent to the British by the French.[12] It was a revolting weapon, but once used by the Germans it was only proper to respond in kind. Far more gas shells needed to be fired at the German front-line dugouts in the hour-long bombardment just prior to the assault. The huge proportion of shells that failed to explode or went off too early would indeed have made a fitting subject for a public inquiry.

Despite actions such as the first day on the Somme and similar bloodbaths (the Battle of Arras saw greater average losses per day than the Battle of the Somme), overall Britain lost proportionately far fewer men killed in the First World War—6.7 per cent of males aged between fourteen and forty-nine—than Germany and Austria at 10 per cent and France at 12.5 per cent.[13] Although the death toll was twice as high in France—the war was fought largely on French soil, and not at all on German— the proportion of servicemen killed in action (one in eight in the British army to one in six in the French) was not so wildly different.[14]

'The British', writes the historian David Reynolds, 'need to remember that the 1st of July 1916 was very unusual in a war that lasted 1,516 days.'[15] Of course if it had not been unusual the war could not have lasted so long, but it had a profound impact on the grand strategy of the Second World War, leaving what a recent historian has correctly called 'a raw psychological wound' on British strategists such as Winston Churchill and FM Sir Alan Brooke.[16] During the Second World War, Churchill and Brooke put off the return to the Continent for four years after the retreat to Dunkirk, preferring to fight in North Africa and Italy than risking a direct assault on France and Germany, in order to avoid a return to the kind of trench warfare seen on the Western Front in the Great War. For all the harsh fighting seen by the British army between 1939 and 1945, none of its men went through anything like the first day of the Somme, even on D-Day.

On campaign in France, a friend of Cpl. James Parr of the 1st/ 16th London Regiment (Queen's Westminster Rifles) asked him why they took the risks they did. Because, he said, 'We could live and love and work somewhere in the world whether Germany or England won. What's the use of it all?' Parr answered him: 'I think we gain the one thing that every man has wanted from his boyhood up—opportunity. Opportunity to show what he is made of. Opportunity to show *himself* what he's made of, to show that he can be a hero...What do we gain? We stand to gain everything and to lose—only our lives.'[17] Parr was killed in action at Gommecourt on the first day of the Somme Offensive, and is buried there alongside 170 of his comrades. He did indeed show himself that he could be a hero, but his death also forced the British army to learn how to win the First World War.

APPENDIX

THE BRITISH INFANTRY
ORDER OF BATTLE
BY BRIGADE & BATTALION,
1 JULY 1916

4th Army
(General Sir Henry Rawlinson)

‖‖‖

III CORPS
(Lt.-Gen. Sir W. P. Pulteney)

....

8th Division (Regular Army)
(Maj.-Gen. H. Hudson)

23rd BRIGADE
—
2nd Devonshire
2nd West Yorkshire
2nd Middlesex
2nd Scottish Rifles

25th BRIGADE
—
2nd Lincoln
2nd Royal Berkshire
1st Royal Irish Rifles
2nd Rifle Brigade

70th BRIGADE
—
11th Sherwood Foresters
8th King's Own Yorkshire Light Infantry
8th Yorkshire and Lancashire
9th Yorkshire and Lancashire

PIONEERS
—
22nd Durham Light Infantry

34th Division (New Army)
(Maj.-Gen. E. C. Ingouville-Williams)

101st BRIGADE

15th Royal Scots (1st Edinburgh City)
16th Royal Scots (2nd Edinburgh City)
10th Lincolnshire (Grimsby Chums)
11th Suffolk (Cambridge)

102nd (TYNESIDE SCOTTISH) BRIGADE

20th Northumberland Fusiliers (1st Tyneside Scottish)
21st Northumberland Fusiliers (2nd Tyneside Scottish)
22nd Northumberland Fusiliers (3rd Tyneside Scottish)
23rd Northumberland Fusiliers (4th Tyneside Scottish)

103rd (TYNESIDE IRISH) BRIGADE

24th Northumberland Fusiliers (1st Tyneside Irish)
25th Northumberland Fusiliers (2nd Tyneside Irish)
26th Northumberland Fusiliers (3rd Tyneside Irish)
27th Northumberland Fusiliers (4th Tyneside Irish)

PIONEERS

18th Northumberland Fusiliers

19th (Western) Division (New Army)
(Maj.-Gen. G. T. M. Bridges)

56th BRIGADE

7th King's Own
7th East Lancashire
7th South Lancashire
7th Loyal North Lancashire

57th BRIGADE

10th Royal Warwickshire
8th Gloucestershire
10th Worcestershire
8th North Staffordshire

58th BRIGADE

9th Cheshire
9th Royal Welch Fusiliers
9th Welch
6th Wiltshire

PIONEERS

5th South Wales Borderers

VIII CORPS
(*Lt.-Gen. Sir A. G. Hunter-Weston*)

4th Division (Regular Army)
(*Maj.-Gen. Hon. W. Lambton*)

10th BRIGADE

1st Royal Irish Fusiliers
2nd Royal Dublin Fusiliers
2nd Seaforth Highlanders
1st Royal Warwickshire

11th BRIGADE

1st Somerset Light Infantry
1st East Lancashire
1st Hampshire
1st Rifle Brigade

12th BRIGADE

1st King's Own
2nd Lancashire Fusiliers
2nd Duke of Wellington's
2nd Essex

PIONEERS

21st West Yorkshire

29th Division (Regular Army)
(Maj.-Gen. H. de Beauvoir de Lisle)

86th BRIGADE
2nd Royal Fusiliers
1st Lancashire Fusiliers
16th Middlesex (Public Schools Battalion)
1st Royal Dublin Fusiliers

87th BRIGADE
2nd South Wales Borderers
1st Kings Own Scottish Borderers
1st Royal Inniskilling Fusiliers
1st Border

88th BRIGADE
1st Essex
1st Newfoundland
4th Worcestershire
2nd Hampshire

PIONEERS
1/2nd Monmouths

31st Division (New Army)
(Maj.-Gen. R. Wanless O'Gowan)

92nd BRIGADE
10th East Yorkshire (Hull Commercials)
11th East Yorkshire (Hull Tradesmen)
12th East Yorkshire (Hull Sportsmen)
13th East Yorkshire (T'Others)

93rd BRIGADE
15th West Yorkshire (Leeds Pals)
16th West Yorkshire (1st Bradford Pals)
18th West Yorkshire (2nd Bradford Pals)
18th Durham Light Infantry (Durham Pals)

94th BRIGADE

11th East Lancashire (Accrington Pals)
12th Yorkshire and Lancashire (Sheffield City Battalion)
13th Yorkshire and Lancashire (1st Barnsley Pals)
14th Yorkshire and Lancashire (1st Barnsley Pals)

PIONEERS

12th King's Own Yorkshire Light Infantry (Halifax Pals)

48th (South Midland) Division (Territorials)
(*Maj.-Gen. R. Fanshaw*)

143th BRIGADE

1/5th Royal Warwickshire
1/6th Royal Warwickshire
1/7th Royal Warwickshire
1/8th Royal Warwickshire

144th BRIGADE

1/4th Gloucestershire
1/6th Gloucestershire
1/7th Worcestershire
1/8th Worcestershire

145th BRIGADE

1/5th Gloucestershire
1/4th Oxford and Buckinghamshire Light Infantry
1st Buckinghamshire
1/4th Royal Berkshire

PIONEERS

1/5th Royal Sussex

X CORPS
(Lt.-Gen. Sir T. L. N. Morland)

....

32nd Division (New Army)
(Maj.-Gen. W.H. Rycroft)

14th BRIGADE

19th Lancashire Fusiliers (3rd Salford Pals)
1st Dorset
2nd Manchester
15th Highland Light Infantry (Glasgow Tramways)

96th BRIGADE

16th Northumberland Fusiliers (Newcastle Commercials)
2nd Royal Inniskilling Fusiliers
15th Lancashire Fusiliers (1st Salford Pals)
16th Lancashire Fusiliers (2nd Salford Pals)

97th BRIGADE

11th Border (The Lonsdales)
2nd King's Own Yorkshire Light Infantry
16th Highland Light Infantry (Glasgow Boys' Brigade)
17th Highland Light Infantry (Glasgow Commercials)

PIONEERS

17th Northumberland Fusiliers (Newcastle Railway Pals)

36th (Ulster) Division (New Army)
(Maj.-Gen. O. S. W. Nugent)

107th BRIGADE

8th Royal Irish Rifles (East Belfast)
9th Royal Irish Rifles (West Belfast)
10th Royal Irish Rifles (South Belfast)
15th Royal Irish Rifles (North Belfast)

Appendix

108th BRIGADE

11th Royal Irish Rifles (South Antrim)
12th Royal Irish Rifles (Central Antrim)
13th Royal Irish Rifles (County Down)
9th Royal Irish Fusiliers (County Armagh, Monaghan and Cavan)

109th BRIGADE

9th Royal Inniskilling Fusiliers (County Tyrone)
10th Royal Inniskilling Fusiliers (County Derry)
11th Royal Inniskilling Fusiliers (Donegal and Fermanagh)
14th Royal Irish Rifles (Belfast Young Citizens)

PIONEERS

16th Royal Irish Rifles (2nd County Down)

49th (West Riding) Division (Territorials)
(*Maj.-Gen. E.M. Perceval*)

146th BRIGADE

1/5th West Yorkshire
1/6th West Yorkshire
1/7th West Yorkshire
1/8th West Yorkshire

147th BRIGADE

1/4th Duke of Wellington's
1/5th Duke of Wellington's
1/6th Duke of Wellington's
1/7th Duke of Wellington's

148th BRIGADE

1/4th Yorkshire and Lancashire
1/5th Yorkshire and Lancashire
1/4th King's Own Yorkshire Light Infantry
1/5th King's Own Yorkshire Light Infantry

PIONEERS

1/3rd Monmouths

XIII CORPS
(Lt.-Gen. W.M. Congreve VC)

....

18th (Eastern) Division (New Army)
(Maj.-Gen. F.I. Maxse)

53rd BRIGADE
—
8th Norfolk
6th Royal Berkshire
10th Essex
8th Suffolk

54th BRIGADE
—
11th Royal Fusiliers
7th Bedfordshire
6th Northamptonshire
12th Middlesex

55th BRIGADE
—
7th Queen's
7th Buffs
8th East Surrey
7th Royal West Kent

PIONEERS
—
8th Royal Sussex

30th Division (New Army)
(Maj.-Gen. J.S.M. Shea)

21st BRIGADE
—
18th King's (2nd Liverpool Pals)
19th Manchester (4th Pals)
2nd Wiltshire
2nd Green Howards

89th BRIGADE

17th King's (1st Liverpool Pals)
19th King's (3rd Liverpool Pals)
20th King's (4th Liverpool Pals)
2nd Bedfordshire

90th BRIGADE

2nd Royal Scots Fusiliers
16th Manchester (1st Pals)
17th Manchester (2nd Pals)
18th Manchester (3rd Pals)

PIONEERS

11th South Lancashire

The 9th (Scottish) Division was in reserve

XV CORPS
(Lt.-Gen. H.S. Horne)

7th Division (Regular Army)
(Maj.-Gen. H.E. Watts)

20th BRIGADE

8th Devonshire
9th Devonshire
2nd Border
2nd Gordon Highlanders

22nd BRIGADE

2nd Royal Warwickshire
20th Manchester (5th Pals)
1st Royal Welch Fusiliers
2nd Royal Irish

91st BRIGADE

2nd Queen's
1st South Staffordshire
21st Manchester (6th Pals)
22nd Manchester (7th Pals)

PIONEERS

24th Manchester (Oldham Pals)

17th (Northern) Division (New Army)
(Maj.-Gen. T.D. Pilcher)

50th BRIGADE

10th West Yorkshire
7th East Yorkshire
7th Green Howards
6th Dorset

51st BRIGADE

7th Lincolnshire
7th Border
8th South Staffordshire
10th Sherwood Foresters

52nd BRIGADE

9th Northumberland Fusiliers
10th Lancashire Fusiliers
9th Duke of Wellington's
12th Manchester

PIONEERS

7th Yorkshire and Lancashire

Appendix

21st Division (New Army)
(*Maj.-Gen. D. G. M. Campbell*)

62nd BRIGADE
12th Northumberland Fusiliers
13th Northumberland Fusiliers
1st Lincolnshire
10th Green Howards

63rd BRIGADE
8th Lincolnshire
8th Somerset Light Infantry
4th Middlesex
10th Yorkshire and Lancashire

64th BRIGADE
9th King's Own Yorkshire Light Infantry
10th King's Own Yorkshire Light Infantry
1st East Yorkshire
15th Durham Light Infantry

PIONEERS
14th Northumberland Fusiliers

3rd Army
(Gen. Sir E. Allenby)

||||||||||||||||||||||||||||||||||||||||||||||||||||||||||||||||||||||||||||||||||||||||||||||||||

VII CORPS
(Lt.-Gen. Sir T. D'Oyly Snow)

46th (North Midland) Division (Territorials)
(Maj.-Gen. Hon E.J. Montagu-Stuart-Wortley)

137th BRIGADE
—
1/5th South Staffordshire
1/6th South Staffordshire
1/5th North Staffordshire
1/6th North Staffordshire

138th BRIGADE
—
1/4th Lincolnshire
1/5th Lincolnshire
1/4th Leicestershire
1/5th Leicestershire

139th BRIGADE
—
1/5th Sherwood Foresters
1/6th Sherwood Foresters
1/7th Sherwood Foresters
1/8th Sherwood Foresters

PIONEERS
—
1/1st Monmouth

Appendix

56th (London) Division (Territorials)
(*Maj.-Gen. C. P. A. Hull*)

167th BRIGADE

1/1st London
1/3rd London
1/7th Middlesex
1/8th Middlesex

168th BRIGADE

1/4th London
1/12th London (Rangers)
1/13th London (Kensington)
1/14th London (1st London Scottish)

169th BRIGADE

1/2nd London
1/5th London (1st London Rifle Brigade)
1/9th London (Queen Victoria's Rifles)
1/16th London (Queen's Westminster Rifles)

PIONEERS

1/5th Cheshire

The 37th Division was in Reserve

SELECT BIBLIOGRAPHY

BOOKS

The bibliography on the battle of the Somme is so vast that I have only
mentioned here books that I have relied on heavily or quoted from in this book.
All books are published in London unless otherwise stated.

ANONYMOUS, *Sixteenth, Seventeenth, Eighteenth, Nineteenth Battalions The
Manchester Regiment: First City Brigade* 1 (Naval and Military Press, 1923)

BARDGETT, Colin, *The Lonsdale Battalion* (The Cromwell Press, 1993)

BARNETT, Correlli, *The Lords of War: Supreme Leadership from Lincoln to
Churchill* (The Praetorian Press, 2012)

BEACH, Jim, *Haig's Intelligence: GHQ and the German Army 1916–1918*
(Cambridge University Press, 2013)

BILTON, David, *Hull Pals* (Wharncliffe Books, 1999)

BLACK, Jeremy, *The Great War and the Making of the Modern World*
(Bloomsbury, 2011)

BLAKE, Robert, (ed.), *The Private Papers of Sir Douglas Haig 1914–1919* (Eyre &
Spottiswoode, 1952)

BOND, Brian, (ed.), et al, *Look To Your Front* (The History Press, 1999)

BORASTON, J. H., (ed.), *Sir Douglas Haig's Despatches* (J.M. Dent & Sons,1919)

BROWN, I. M., *British Logistics on the Western Front 1914–19* (Praeger Publishers,
Connecticut, 1998)

BRYANT, Peter, *Grimsby Chums* (Humberside Heritage Publications, 1990)

CARTER, Terry, *Birmingham Pals* (Pen & Sword, 1997)

CAVE, Nigel, *Battleground Europe: Somme* (Pen & Sword, 2000)

CHARTERIS, John, *Field-Marshal Earl Haig* (Cassell, 1929)

——, *At G.H.Q.* (Cassell, 1931)

CHRISTIE, N.M., *For King and Empire: The Newfoundlanders in the Great War*
(CEF Books, Ottawa, 2003)

CHURCHILL, Winston, *The World Crisis,* vol 3 (Thornton Butterfield, 1927)

——, *Great Contemporaries* (Macmillan and Co., 1942)

COOKSEY, Jon, *Pals: The 13th and 14th Battalions York and Lancaster Regiments*
(Barnsley Chronicle, 1986)

COOPER, Alfred Duff, *Haig* (Faber, 1935)

COWLEY, Robert, (ed.), *The Great War: Perspectives on the Great War* (Random House, 2004)

DEWAR, George, and Boraston, J.H., *Sir Douglas Haig's Command* (Constable, 1922)

DUFFY, Christopher, *The German Army on the Somme* (Pen & Sword, 2007)

EDMONDS, Brig-Gen. Sir J.E., *Military Operations: France and Belgium 1916*, vol 1, 1932

EMDEN, Richard Van, *Meeting the Enemy* (Bloomsbury, 2013)

——, *Tommy's War* (Bloomsbury, 2014)

ENGLUND, Peter, *The Beauty and the Sorrow: An Intimate History of the First World War* (Knopf, 2011)

FARRAR-HOCKLEY, A.H., *The Somme* (Batsford, 1964)

FERGUSON, Niall, *The Pity of War* (Basic Books, 1999)

GIBSON, Ralph, and Oldfield, Paul, *Sheffield City Battalion* (Leo Cooper, 1988)

GILBERT, Martin, *The Somme* (Henry Holt & Co., 2006)

HAIG, Countess, *The Man I Knew* (Moray Press, 1936)

HARRIS, John, *Covenant with Death* (Arrow, 1961)

HART, Peter, *The Somme* (Cassell Military Paperbacks, 2008)

HASTINGS, Max, *Catastrophe: Europe Goes to War 1914* (William Collins, 2013)

HERWIG, H.H., *First World War* (Bloomsbury, 1997)

HORNE, Charles, F., (ed.), *Sources Records of The Great War*, vol. 4 (The American Legion, Indianapolis, 1931)

JÜNGER, Ernst, *Storm of Steel* (Allen Lane, 2003)

KEEGAN, John, *The Face of Battle* (Penguin, 1976)

——, *The First World War* (Alfred A. Knopf, 2001)

LEE, John, *The Warlords: Hindenburg and Ludendorff* (Weidenfeld & Nicolson, 2005)

LEWIS, Cecil, *Sagittarius Rising* (Greenhill, 1936)

LEWIS, John, (ed.), *The Mammoth Book of How it Happened* (Robinson, 1998)

LIDDELL HART, B.H., *Through the Fog of War* (Random House, 1938)

LLOYD GEORGE, D., *War Memoirs* (Odhams, 1931)

LUDENDORFF, Erich, *My War Memories*, vol. I (Hutchinson, 1919)

MCCARTHY, Chris, *The Somme: The Day-by-Day Account* (Greenwich Editions, 1996)

MACDONALD, Alan, *Z Day: The Attack of the VIII Corps at Beaumont Hamel and Serre* (Iona, 2014)

MACE, Martin, and GREHAN, John, (eds.), *Slaughter on the Somme: The Complete War Diaries of the British Army's Worst Day* (Pen & Sword, 2013)

MADDOCKS, Graham, *Liverpool Pals* (Pen & Sword, 1991)

MAYHEW, Emily, *Wounded: A New History of the Western Front in World War I* (Oxford University Press, 2014)

MEAD, Gary, *The Good Soldier: The Biography of Douglas Haig* (Atlantic, 2007)

——, *Victoria's Cross* (Atlantic, 2014)

MIDDLEBROOK, Martin, *The First Day on the Somme* (Penguin, 2001)

MILNER, Laurie, *Leeds Pals* (Pen & Sword, 1991)

NICHOLS, G.H.F., *The 18th Division in the Great War* (William Blackwood, 1922)

NICHOLSON, G.W.L., *The Fighting Newfoundlander* (McGill-Queens University Press, 2006)

PHILPOTT, William, *Bloody Victory: The Sacrifice on the Somme* (Little, Brown, 2009)

——, *War of Attrition: Fighting the First World War* (Overlook Press, 2014)

PRIOR, Robin and WILSON, Trevor, *Command on the Western Front: Military Career of Sir Henry Rawlinson, 1914–1918* (Blackwell, 1992)

RAWSON, Andy, *Somme Campaign* (Pen & Sword, 2014)

REYNOLDS, David, *The Long Shadow: The Legacies of the Great War in the Twentieth Century* (Simon & Schuster, 2014)

ROBERTSHAW, Andrew, *Somme 1 July 1916* (Osprey, 2006)

ROGERSON, Sidney, *Twelve Days on the Somme* (Greenhill, 2006)

SASSOON, Siegfried, *Memoirs of an Infantry Officer* (Faber, 1965)

SELDON, Anthony, and WALSH, David, *Public Schools and the Great War* (Pen & Sword, 2014)

SHEEN, John, *Tyneside Irish* (Pen & Sword, 1998)

SHEFFIELD, Gary, *Forgotten Victory—The First World War: Myths and Realities* Hodder Headline, 2001

——, *The Somme* (Cassell, 2003)

SHEFFIELD, Gary, and BOURNE, John, (eds.), *Douglas Haig: War Diaries and Letters 1914–1918* (Weidenfeld & Nicolson, 2005)

SHELDON, Jack, *The German Army on the Somme* (Pen & Sword, 2007)

STEDMAN, Michael, *Salford Pals* (Pen & Sword, 1993)

——, *Manchester Pals* (Pen & Sword, 1994)

STEVENSON, David, *1914–1918: A History of the First World War* (Allen Lane, 2004)

STEWART, Graham, and SHEEN, John, *Tyneside Scottish* (Pen & Sword, 1999)

STRACHAN, Hew, *The First World War: A New History* (Simon & Schuster, 2014)

TERRAINE, John, *Douglas Haig: The Educated Soldier* (Hutchinson, 1963)

TRAVERS, Tim, *Killing Ground: The British Army, the Western Front and the Emergence of Modern Warfare 1900–1918* (Harper Collins, 1987)

TURNER, William, *Accrington Pals* (Pen & Sword, 1993)

WATSON, Alexander, *Ring of Steel: Germany and Austria in World War I* (Basic Civitas, 2014)

WILLIAMSON, Henry, *The Golden Virgin* (Faber, 2010)

WINTER, Jay, *The Great War and the British People* (Macmillan, 1986)

WINTER, Michael, *Into the Blizzard: Walking the Fields of the Newfoundland Dead* (Doubleday, 2014)

ARTICLES

BOURNE, John, 'The BEF on the Somme: Some Career Aspects. Part 1, 1 July 1916', from *Gun Fire. A Journal of First World War History*, No. 35, pp. 2–14 (York, 1996)

GREENHALGH, Elizabeth, 'Why the British were on the Somme in 1916', *War in History* 6, pp. 147-73 (California, 1999)

——, 'Flames on the Somme', *War in History* 10, pp. 335–42 (California, 2003)

LEE, John, 'Some Lessons of the Somme', in ed. Bond, Brian et al, *Look To Your Front,* 1999

MARBLE, Sandars, 'Wire Cutting on the Somme' *Stand To!*, No. 61 (Staplehurst, April 2001)

PHILPOTT, William, 'Why the British Were Really on the Somme', *War in History* 9, pp. 446–71 (California, 2002)

PUGSLEY, Christopher, 'Haig and the Implementation of Tactical Doctrine on the Western Front', *Sandhurst Occasional Paper,* No. 8 (Sandhurst, 1991)

STRACHAN, Hew, 'The Battle of the Somme and British Strategy' *Journal of Strategic Studies*, No. 21, pp. 79–85 (Oxford, 1998)

SYM, Andrew, 'The Learning Curve: The 46th North Midland Division on the Western Front', *History Today*, November 2004 (London)

NOTES TO THE TEXT

INTRODUCTION

1 Nicholson, *The Fighting Newfoundlander*, p. 269.
2 Cave, *Battleground Europe*, p. 58.
3 Nicholson, *The Fighting Newfoundlander*, p. 543.
4 Cave, *Battleground Europe*, p. 58.
5 Christie, *For King and Empire*, p. 14.
6 Ibid., p. 20.
7 Christie, *For King and Empire*, pp. 20–1.
8 Nicholson, *The Fighting Newfoundlander*, p. 270.
9 Ibid., p. 261.
10 Ibid., p. 261 n. 1.
11 Mace and Grehan (eds.), *Slaughter on the Somme*, p. 93.
12 Nicholson, *The Fighting Newfoundlander*, p. 268.
13 Christie, *For King and Empire*, p. 15.
14 Cave, *Battleground Europe*, pp. 62–3.
15 MacDonald, *Z Day*, p. 614.
16 Cave, *Battleground Europe*, p. 58.
17 Christie, *For King and Empire*, p. 21.
18 Nicholson, *The Fighting Newfoundlander*, p. 271.
19 Christie, *For King and Empire*, p. 21.
20 Cowley (ed.), *Great War*, p. 326.
21 Mace and Grehan (eds.), *Slaughter on the Somme*, p. 141.
22 Christie, *For King and Empire*, p. 33.
23 Ibid., p. 21.
24 Nicholson, *The Fighting Newfoundlander*, pp. 272–3.
25 Mace and Grehan (eds.), *Slaughter on the Somme*, p. 141.
26 Nicholson, *The Fighting Newfoundlander*, p. 272.
27 Mace and Grehan (eds.), *Slaughter on the Somme*, p. 141.
28 Ibid., p. 142.
29 Ibid., p. 141.
30 Cave, *Battleground Europe*, p. 67.
31 Ibid.
32 Ibid.
33 MacDonald, *Z Day*, pp. 614–15.
34 Ibid., p. 610 n. 1.
35 Christie, *For King and Empire*, p. 19.
36 Sheffield, *Somme*, p. 50.
37 Winter, *Into the Blizzard*, p. 18.
38 Ibid., p. 24.
39 Christie, *For King and Empire*, p. 21.
40 Cave, *Battleground Europe*, p. 74.

CHAPTER ONE

1 Mead, *Victoria's Cross*, p. 126.
2 Middlebrook, *The First Day*, p. 316.

3 Sheffield and Bourne (eds.), *Haig's War Diaries and Letters*, p. 171.

4 Clark, *The Donkeys: A History of the British Expeditionary Force in 1915* (1961).

5 Barnett, *The Lords of War*, p. 88.

6 Sheffield, *The Chief*, p. 151

7 Keegan, *The First World War*, p. 267.

8 Churchill, *Great Contemporaries*, p. 165.

9 Ibid., p. 169.

10 *London Review of Books*, Vol. 13, No. 8 (25 April 1991).

11 Keegan, *The First World War*, p. 267.

12 Sheffield and Bourne (eds.), *Haig's War Diaries and Letters*, p. 217.

13 Barnett, *The Lords of War*, p. 85.

14 National Archives WO95/863.

15 Barnett, *The Lords of War*, p. 85.

16 Ibid., p. 87.

17 Sheffield, *The Somme*, p. 12.

18 Keegan, *The Face of Battle*, p. 211.

19 Watson, *Ring of Steel*, p. 311.

20 *The Western Front Association Bulletin*, No. 76 (Oct/Nov 2006), p. 12.

21 Richard Holmes in Sheffield, *The Somme*, p. ix.

22 Sheffield., *The Somme*, p. 15.

23 Keegan, *The Face of Battle*, p. 213.

24 Sheffield and Bourne (eds.), *Haig's War Diaries and Letters*, p. 188.

25 Barnett, *The Lords of War*, p. 91.

26 Keegan, *The Face of Battle*, p. 206.

27 Barnett, *The Lords of War*, p. 91.

28 Watson, *Ring of Steel*, p. 315.

29 Bourne, 'The BEF on the Somme', pp. 2–14.

30 Charteris, *At G.H.Q*, p. 151.

31 Keegan, *The Face of Battle*, p. 210.

32 Watson, *Ring of Steel*, p. 312.

33 *The Western Front Association Bulletin*, No. 76, p. 12.

34 Watson, *Ring of Steel*, p. 313.

35 Cowley (ed.), *Great War*, p. 324.

36 MacDonald, *Z Day*, pp. 614–15.

37 Keegan, *The First World War*, p. 267.

38 Prior and Wilson, *Command on the Western Front*, p. 139.

39 Keegan, *The Face of Battle*, p. 209.

40 Ibid.

41 IWM 6847, 195/2882, p. 25.

42 Harris, *Covenant with Death*, p. 44.

43 Reynolds, *The Long Shadow*, p. 414.

44 Harris, *Covenant with Death*, p. 61.

45 IWM 3834, 85/51/1.

46 Christie, *For King and Empire*, p. 8.

47 Watson, *Ring of Steel*, p. 314.

48 Bourne, 'The BEF on the Somme', pp. 2–14.

49 Ibid.

CHAPTER TWO

1 Middlebrook, *The First Day*, p. 315.

2 Ibid.

3 Barnett, *The Lords of War*, p. 91.

4 Keegan, *The First World War*, p. 269.

5 Sheffield, *The Somme*, p. 22.

6 Sheffield, *The Somme*, p. 40; MacDonald, *Z Day*, p. 615.

7 Herwig, *First World War*, p. 313.

8 Watson, *Ring of Steel*, p. 312.

9 Cowley (ed.), *Great War*, p. 329.

10 Ibid., p.328.

11 Ibid., p. 324.

12 Liddell Hart, *Through the Fog of War*, p. 258

13 Ibid., p. 328.

14 Herwig, *First World War*, p. 313.

15 Ibid.

16 Stevenson, *1914–1918*, p. 169.

17 Haig, *The Man I Knew*, p. 159.

18 Beach, *Haig's Intelligence*, p. 197.

19 Sheffield and Bourne (eds.), *Haig's War Diaries and Letters*, p. 191

20 Cowley (ed.), *Great War*, p. 336.

21 Ibid., p. 323.

22 Pugsley, p. 5.

23 Marble, 'Wire Cutting', *Stand To!*, pp. 36–9.

24 Cowley (ed.), *Great War*, p. 328.

25 Watson, *Ring of Steel*, p. 311.

26 Keegan, *Face of Battle*, pp. 238–40.

27 Beach, *Haig's Intelligence*, p. 196.

28 Ibid., p. 322.

29 Sheffield, *The Somme*, p. 34.

30 Marble, 'Wire Cutting', *Stand To!*.

31 Edmonds, *Military Operations*, p. 485.

32 MacDonald, *Z Day*, p. 620.

33 Beach, *Haig's Intelligence*, p. 324.

34 Ibid., p. 322.

35 Ibid., p. 199.

36 Ibid., p. 200.

37 Sassoon, *Memoirs of an Infantry Officer*, p. 45.

38 Sheffield and Bourne (eds.), *Haig's War Diaries and Letters*, 16 June 1916.

39 *The Western Front Association Bulletin*, No. 76, p. 12.

40 Beach, *Haig's Intelligence*, p. 201.

41 Charteris, John, *At G.H.Q* (1931)

42 Ibid.

43 Sassoon, *Memoirs of an Infantry Officer*, p. 30.

44 Ibid., pp. 32–3.

45 Ibid., p. 35.

46 Ibid., p. 45.

47 Sheffield, *The Somme*, p. 27.

48 Nicholson, *The Fighting Newfoundlander*, p. 252.

49 Ibid.; Horne (ed.), *Source Records* Vol. 4, p. 244.

50 Ibid.

51 Hastings, *Catastrophe*, p. 338.

52 Philpott, *Bloody Victory*, p. 464.

53 Strachan, *First World War*, p. 286.

CHAPTER THREE

1 Nichols, *The 18th Division*, p. 36.

2 Edmonds, *Military Operations*, p. vii.

3 IWM 7990, 82/1/1, pp. 52–60.

4 Ibid.

5 Ibid.

6 Ibid.

7 Edmonds, *Military Operations*, p. 315.

8 Sheffield, *The Somme*, p. 35.

9 Ibid., p. 36.

10 Harris, *Covenant with Death*, p. 315.

11 IWM 17105, 09/47/1.
12 Emden, *Tommy's War*, p. 209.
13 Ibid.
14 Nichols, *The 18th Division*, p. 37.
15 Brown, *British Logistics*, p. 125.
16 Emden, *Tommy's War*, p. 210.
17 Ibid., p. 211.
18 Watson, *Ring of Steel*, p. 316.
19 Englund, *The Beauty and the Sorrow*, p. 498.
20 Stewart and Sheen, *Tyneside Scottish*, p. 96.
21 Sheffield, *The Somme*, p. 36.
22 Mead, *Victoria's Cross*, p. 127.
23 Stevenson, *1914–1918*, p. 170.
24 Edmonds, *Military Operations*, p. 486.
25 Watson, *Ring of Steel*, p. 316.
26 Ibid.
27 Middlebrook, *The First Day*, p. 88.
28 Barnett, *Lords of War*, p. 101.
29 Keegan, *The Face of Battle*, p. 205.
30 IWM 8600, 99/56/1.
31 IWM 8600, 99/56/1.
32 Watson, *Ring of Steel*, p. 317.
33 MacDonald, *Z Day*, p. 620.
34 Ibid., p. 621.
35 Watson, *Ring of Steel*, p. 317.
36 Horne (ed.), *Source Records*, Vol. 4, p. 243.
37 Ibid.
38 Edmonds, *Military Operations*, p. 485.
39 Stevenson, *1914–1918*, p. 169.
40 Harris, *Covenant with Death*, p. 209.
41 Edmonds, *Military Operations*, p. 461.
42 Watson, *Ring of Steel*, p. 313.
43 Jünger, *Storm of Steel*, p. 76.
44 Marble, 'Wire cutting', *Stand To!*, pp. 36–9.
45 Ibid.
46 Ibid., *passim*.
47 Keegan, *The First World War*, p. 269.
48 Marble, 'Wire cutting", *Stand To!*, pp. 36–9.
49 Sassoon, *Memoirs of an Infantry Officer*, p. 49.
50 Ibid., p. 51.
51 Stevenson, *1914–1918*, p. 169.
52 Horne (ed.), *Source Records*, Vol. 4, p. 246.
53 Reynolds, *The Long Shadow*, p. 333.
54 Horne (ed.), *Source Records*, Vol. 4, p. 246.
55 Ibid., p. 248.
56 Jünger, *Storm of Steel*, pp. 76–7.
57 Englund, *The Beauty and the Sorrow*, p. 273.
58 Emden, *Tommy's War*, pp. 215–16.
59 IWM 8600, 99/56/1.
60 Emden, *Tommy's War*, p. 216.
61 Ibid.
62 IWM 7990, 82/1/1, pp. 52–60.
63 IWM 4910, 96/17/1.
64 Emden, *Tommy's War*, p. 217.
65 IWM 12105, 66/96/1.
66 Ibid., p. 10.
67 Ibid., p. 11.
68 Sassoon, *Memoirs of an Infantry Officer*, p. 46.
69 Bardgett, *Lonsdale Battalion*, p. 23.
70 Sassoon, *Memoirs of an Infantry Officer*, p. 30.

71 Ibid., p. 45.

72 IWM 4910, 96/17/1.

73 IWM 7990, 82/1/1 pp. 52–60.

74 Ibid.

75 Ibid.

76 Sassoon, *Memoirs of an Infantry Officer*, p. 41.

77 Emden, *Tommy's War*, p. 218.

78 IWM 4910, 96/17/1.

79 Emden, *Tommy's War*, p. 220.

80 Sassoon, *Memoirs of an Infantry Officer*, p. 45.

81 Cowley (ed.), *Great War*, p. 123.

CHAPTER FOUR

1 Middlebrook, *The First Day on the Somme*, p. 104. Poem published two days before the Somme Offensive, in which Hodgson was killed at Mametz aged twenty-three.

2 IWM 12105, 66/96/1, p. 12.

3 Sassoon, *Memoirs of an Infantry Officer*, p. 53.

4 IWM 7990, 82/1/1, pp. 52–60.

5 Nichols, *The 18th Division*, p. 38.

6 IWM 11597 01/45/1.

7 Edmonds, *Military Operations*, p. 485.

8 Ibid., p. 315.

9 Emden, *Tommy's War*, pp. 219–20.

10 Sheffield, *The Somme*, p. 40.

11 IWM 11597, 01/45/1.

12 Ibid.

13 IWM 11597 01/45/1.

14 Nicholson, *The Fighting Newfoundlander*, p. 259.

15 MacDonald, *Z Day*, p. 617.

16 Edmonds, *Military Operations*, p. 313.

17 Edmonds, *Military Operations*, p. 314, n.1.

18 Stewart and Sheen, *Tyneside Scottish*, p. 95.

19 Mayhew, *Wounded*, p. 74.

20 Cowley (ed.), *Great War*, p. 337.

21 IWM 8600, 99/56/1.

22 Nicholson, *The Fighting Newfoundlanders*, pp. 265–6.

23 MacDonald, *Z Day*, p. 607.

24 Ibid., p. 616.

25 Stewart and Sheen, *Tyneside Scottish*, p. 97.

26 Cowley (ed.), *Great War*, p. 323.

27 Stewart and Sheen, *Tyneside Scottish*, p. 98.

28 Cowley (ed.), *Great War*, p. 337.

29 Nichols, *The 18th Division*, p. 38.

30 Middlebrook, *The First Day*, p. 121.

31 IWM 4910, 96/17/1.

32 Andrew Stuttaford in *The New Criterion*, Vol. 33, No. 2 (October 2014), p. 11.

33 Middlebrook, *The First Day*, p. 87.

34 Nichols, *The 18th Division*, p. 38.

35 Cowley (ed.), *Great War*, p. 323.

36 Middlebrook, *The First Day*, p. 58.

37 Ibid., p. 125.

38 Ibid., p. 156.

39 Ibid., p. 123.

40 Ibid.

41 Ibid., p. 316.

42 Cowley (ed.), *Great War*, p. 327.

43 Ibid., p. 326.

44 Ibid., pp. 327–8.
45 Harris, *Covenant with Death*, p. 441.
46 Edmonds, *Military Operations*, pp. 392–3.
47 MacDonald, *Z Day*, p. 618.
48 Ibid.
49 Middlebrook, *The First Day*, p. 128.
50 Ibid., p. 184.
51 Horne (ed.), *Source Records* IV, p. 246.
52 Churchill, *World Crisis*, Vol. 3, Part 1, p. 195.
53 Mead, *Victoria's Cross*, p. 124.
54 Middlebrook, *The First Day*, Appendix 4, pp. 317–24.
55 Mead, *Victoria's Cross*, p. 138.
56 Ibid., p. 133.
57 Ibid., p. 138.
58 Middlebrook, *The First Day*, p. 129.
59 Edmonds, *Military Operations*, p. 393.
60 Middlebrook, *The First Day*, p. 148.
61 Ibid., p. 163.
62 Mead, *Victoria's Cross*, p. 131.
63 Lewis (ed.), *Mammoth Book*, p. 336.
64 Ibid.
65 IWM 17105, 09/47/1.
66 Jünger, *Storm of Steel*, p .53.
67 Ibid., p. 54.
68 Ibid., p58.
69 Ibid., pp. 58–9.
70 Ibid., p. 63.
71 Ibid., p. 71.
72 Ibid., p. 80.
73 Ibid., p. 84.

CHAPTER FIVE

1 Middlebrook, *The First Day*, p. 134.
2 Sheffield and Bourne (ed.), *Haig's War Diaries and Letters*, p. 195.
3 Sym, 'Learning Curve', p. 13.
4 Edmonds, *Military Operations*, p. 461.
5 Sheffield and Bourne (ed.), *Haig's War Diaries and Letters*, p. 196.
6 Sym, 'Learning Curve', p. 13.
7 Sheffield, *The Somme*, p. 37.
8 IWM 7990, 82/1/1, pp. 52–60.
9 Ibid.
10 Ibid.
11 Ibid.
12 Edmonds, *Military Operations*, p. 485.
13 Ibid., p. 485.
14 Sheffield, *The Somme*, p. 47.
15 Middlebrook, *The First Day*, p. 151.
16 Harris, *Covenant with Death*, p. 500.
17 *The Western Front Association Bulletin*, No. 76, p. 12.
18 Sheffield, *The Somme*, p. 48.
19 Middlebrook, *The First Day*, p. 134.
20 Christie, *For King and Empire*, p. 13.
21 MacDonald, *Z Day*, p. 618.
22 Nicholson, *The Fighting Newfoundlanders*, p. 267.

23 Edmonds, *Military Operations*, p. 404.
24 Ibid., p. 405.
25 Sheffield, *The Somme*, p. 51.
26 IWM 6477, 97/16/1.
27 Ibid.
28 Edmonds, *Military Operations*, p. 400.
29 Sheffield, *The Somme*, p. 51.
30 Edmonds, *Military Operations*, p. 400.
31 Cowley (ed.), *Great War*, p. 326.
32 Bardgett, *Lonsdale Battalion*, p. 20.
33 Ibid., p. 21.
34 Ibid., p. 24.
35 Ibid.
36 Ibid., p. 27.
37 Ibid.
38 Ibid.
39 Ibid., p. 22.
40 Ibid., p. 28.
41 Sheffield, *The Somme*, p. 52.
42 Bryant, *Grimsby Chums*, p. 56.
43 Ibid.
44 Ibid., p. 57–8.
45 Ibid., p. 59.
46 Ibid., p. 67.
47 Stewart and Sheen, *Tyneside Scottish*, p. 8.
48 Ibid., p. 99.
49 Ibid.
50 Ibid.
51 Ibid., p. 101.
52 Ibid.
53 Ibid.
54 Ibid., p. 104.
55 Ibid.
56 Ibid.
57 Ibid., p. 106.
58 Ibid., p. 107.
59 Ibid., p. 108.
60 Cowley (ed.), *Great War*, p. 325.
61 Sheffield, *The Somme*, p. 59.
62 IWM 7397, 76/226/1, Letterbook, p. 19.
63 IWM 7397, 76/226/1, Letterbook, pp. 22–3.
64 Cowley (ed.), *Great War*, p. 336.
65 IWM 4910, 96/17/1.
66 Sheffield and Bourne (eds.), *Haig's War Diaries and Letters*, p. 195.
67 Keegan, *The First World War*, p. 270.
68 Cowley (ed.), *Great War*, p. 330.
69 Horne (ed.), *Source Records* IV, p. 246.
70 Robertshaw, *Somme*, p. 67.
71 IWM 8600, 99/56/1.
72 Ibid.
73 Brooke, Rupert, 'Finding', in *Collected Poems*, (New York: John Lane, 1916).
74 Sheffield, *The Somme*, p. 59.
75 Nichols, *The 18th Division*, p. 43.
76 Edmonds, *Military Operations*, p. 345, n.1.
77 Nichols, *The 18th Division*, p. 42.
78 Sheffield, *The Somme*, p. 64.
79 Cowley (ed.), *Great War*, p. 332.
80 IWM 11597, 01/45/1.
81 Ibid.
82 Edmonds, *Military Operations*, p. 342
83 Cowley (ed.), *Great War*, p. 330.
84 Sheffield, *The Somme*, p. 65.

85 Edmonds, *Military Operations*, p. 343.
86 Ibid.
87 Cowley (ed.), *Great War*, p. 328.
88 Haig, *The Man I Knew*, p. 160.
89 Sheffield and Bourne (eds.), *Haig's War Diaries and Letters*, p. 196.
90 *Times Literary Supplement*, 16 September 2005, p. 4.
91 Haig, *The Man I Knew*, p. 159.
92 MacDonald, *Z Day*, p. 609.
93 Ibid., p. 607.
94 Bourne, 'The BEF on the Somme', pp. 2–14.

CHAPTER SIX

1 Roberts, Andrew (ed.), *Letters from the Front* (2014), p. 79.
2 Middlebrook, *The First Day*, p. 229.
3 Harris, *Covenant with Death*, pp. 478–9.
4 Bardgett, *Lonsdale Battalion*, p. 30.
5 Edmonds, *Military Operations*, p. 483; Mace and Grehan (eds.), *Slaughter on the Somme* p. x.
6 Mace and Grehan (eds.), *Slaughter on the Somme*, p. x.
7 Middlebrook, *The First Day*, Appendix 5, p. 331.
8 Haig, *The Man I Knew*, p. 160.
9 Cowley (ed.), *Great War*, p. 326.
10 Max Hastings, *Catastrophe*, p. 181.
11 Middlebrook, *The First Day*, p. 316.
12 Edmonds, *Military Operations*, p. 484.
13 Stewart and Sheen, *Tyneside Scottish*, p. 107.
14 Middlebrook, *The First Day*, p. 328.
15 Stevenson, *1914–1918*, p. 170.
16 Mace and Grehan (eds.), *Slaughter on the Somme*, p. x.
17 Reynolds, *The Long Shadow*, p. 335.
18 *The Western Front Association Bulletin*, No 76, p. 12.
19 Englund, *The Beauty and the Sorrow*, p. 300. f.78.
20 Reynolds, *The Long Shadow*, p. 336.
21 Ibid., p. 335.
22 Mayhew, *Wounded*, pp. 1–7.
23 Ibid., p. 168.
24 Ibid.
25 Ibid., p. 52.
26 Ibid.
27 Ibid., p. 74.
28 Ibid., p. 78.
29 Ibid., p. 79.
30 Emden, *Meeting the Enemy*, p. 195.
31 Keegan, *The First World War*, pp. 275–6.
32 Keegan, *The First World War*, p. 276.
33 Emden, *Meeting the Enemy*, p. 195.
34 Ibid.
35 Ibid.
36 Ibid., pp. 196–7.
37 IWM 11597, 01/45/1.
38 Emden, *Meeting the Enemy*, pp. 198–9.

39 Emden, *Meeting the Enemy*, p. 199.
40 Sheffield and Bourne (eds.), *Haig's War Diaries and Letters*, p. 197.
41 Ibid.
42 Ibid.
43 IWM 4910, 96/17/1.
44 Mace and Grehan (eds.), *Slaughter on the Somme*, p. x.
45 Barnett, *The Lords of War*, p. 92.
46 Ludendorff, *War Memories*, vol. I, p. 307.
47 Beach, *Haig's Intelligence*, p. 203.
48 Edmonds, *Military Operations*, p. 319.
49 Bourne, 'The BEF on the Somme', pp. 2–14.
50 Ibid.
51 Ibid.
52 Stevenson, *1914–1918*, p. 170.
53 Horne (ed.), *Source Records*, vol. 4, p. 246.
54 Stevenson, *1914–1918*, p. 170.
55 Gilbert, *Somme*, pp. 186–8.
56 Horne (ed.), *Source Records*, vol. 4, p. 252.
57 Mace and Grehan (eds.), *Slaughter on the Somme*, p. ix.
58 Englund, *The Beauty and the Sorrow*, pp. 306–7.
59 Nigel Jones in *Literary Review* (July 2006), p. 12.
60 Keegan, *The First World War*, p. 280.
61 Ibid., p. 274.
62 Jay Winter in *Times Literary Supplement* (16 June 2006), p. 14.
63 *The Western Front Association Bulletin*, No 76, p. 12.
64 Churchill, *Great Contemporaries*, p. 167.
65 Barnett, *The Lords of War*, p. 89.
66 Ibid., p. 104.
67 Emden, *Meeting the Enemy*, p. 208.
68 Stevenson, *1914–1918*, p. 171.
69 Ibid.

CHAPTER SEVEN

1 Edmonds, *Military Operations*, p. vi.
2 Jünger, *Storm of Steel*, p. 69.
3 MacDonald, *Z Day*, p. 608.
4 Richard Holmes in Sheffield, *The Somme*, p. x.
5 MacDonald, *Z Day*, p. 620.
6 Reynolds, *The Long Shadows*, p. 356.
7 MacDonald, *Z Day*, p. 611.
8 National Archives WO95/863.
9 Keegan, *The First World War*, p. 270.
10 *The Western Front Association Bulletin*, No. 76, p. 12.
11 IWM 8600, 99/56/1.
12 Jünger, *Storm of Steel*, p. 78.
13 Mace and Grehan (eds.), *Slaughter on the Somme*, p. 92.
14 Barnett, *The Lords of War*, p. 91.
15 Lee, 'Some Lessons', p. 80.
16 Ibid., p. 81.
17 Sym, 'Learning Curve', p. 15.
18 Lee, 'Some Lessons', p. 81.
19 Ibid., p. 84.

20 Ibid., p. 86.
21 MacDonald, *Z Day*, p. 616.
22 Ibid., p. 618.
23 Richard Holmes in Sheffield, *The Somme*, p. ix.
24 Sheffield, *The Somme* p. x
25 Sheffield, *The Chief*, p. 380.
26 Barnett, *The Lords of War*, p. 136.
27 Ibid.

CONCLUSION

1 Middlebrook, *The First Day*, p. 315.
2 Ibid., p. 316.
3 Keegan, *The First World War*, p. 280.
4 Sheffield, *The Somme*, p. 155.
5 Barnett, *The Lords of War*, p. 83.
6 Gilbert, *Somme*, p. 115.
7 Ibid., pp. 221–2.

8 Edmonds, *Military Operations*, p. 484.
9 Ibid.
10 Nigel Jones in *Literary Review* (July 2006), p. 12.
11 Edmonds, *Military Operations*, p. 486.
12 Ibid.
13 Barnett, *The Lords of War*, p. 96.
14 Jay Winter in *Times Literary Supplement* (16 June 2006), p. 15.
15 Reynolds, *Long Shadows*, p. 424.
16 Barnett, *The Lords of War*, p. 292.
17 Emden, *Tommy's War*, p. 365.

APPENDIX:
ORDER OF BATTLE

Details for this chapter taken from Middlebrook, *The First Day*, pp. 317–24.

INDEX

Index

ACKNOWLEDGEMENTS

I should very much like to thank for all their help Sir Peter Ricketts for allowing me to work in the Duff Cooper Library in the British Embassy in Paris; Peter Hart and Belinda Haley at the Imperial War Museum Library and Archive; William Birch for historical research; Avril Williams for showing me the Great War graffiti in her cellars in Auchonvillers; my daughter Cassia Roberts for the story of Horace Iles from her trip to the Somme; the Commonwealth War Graves Commission for the wonderful work it does; David Rakowski for showing me the Glory Hole at La Boisselle; the staff of the London Library, where the First World War is still called 'European War (I)'; John Lee and Zhelun Chen for reading the book at proof stage, and especially the historians Chris McCarthy and Simon Jones for their advice and for explaining the workings of the 106 fuse to me, using a Brooks's Club bread roll.

I would like to thank Anthony Cheetham whose idea this book was, Neil Belton, and Georgina Blackwell at Head of Zeus, as well as my agent Georgina Capel of Georgina Capel Associates, for their customary superb professionalism.

This book is dedicated to John Lee in profound thanks for all the battlefield touring we've done together, and for all the completely invaluable help he has given me in this and others of my works. For this book alone we toured the Lochnagar Crater, Beaumont-Hamel British Cemetery, Thiepval Memorial to the Missing and the Thiepval Anglo-French Cemetery, Leipzig Redoubt, Pozières British Cemetery, Cléry-sur-Somme Nécropole Nationale, Dantzig Alley British Cemetery, Devonshire Cemetery Mansell Copse, Deutscher Soldatenhof Fricourt, Musée Somme in Albert, Orvillers British Cemetery, Schwaben Redoubt, Connaught Cemetery, Mill Road Cemetery, Newfoundland War Memorial Park at Beaumont Hamel, Y Ravine Cemetery, Hunters Cemetery, Hawthorn Ridge Cemetery No.2, Bapaume Post Military Cemetery, Serre Road Cemetery Nos.1, 2 and 3, Serre-Hébuterne Nécropole Nationale, Railway Hollow Cemetery, Sheffield Memorial Park, Railway Hollow Cemetery, Queen's Cemetery, Luke Copse British Cemetery, Gommecourt Wood New Cemetery and Gommecourt British Cemetery No 2. I would also like to thank John's wife Celia Lee and my wife Susan Gilchrist for showing such forbearance as we disappear so often and for so long over the years.

I would particularly like to thank John for pointing out to me—just before I was moronically about to pick them up—that two 18lb and 6″ shells lying on a track just off the Serre-Hébuterne road still had their fuses inside, and were thus part of the 'Iron Harvest' of unexploded ordnance.

ANDREW ROBERTS
January 2015
www.andrew-roberts.net

LIST OF ILLUSTRATIONS

List of Illustrations

A note on the Types

The text typeface is
MONOTYPE EHRHARDT,
a digital recutting of a face
originally designed for
metal composition and issued
by Monotype in 1938.
One of several modern
derivatives of types
cut in Amsterdam, *c.*1690
by Hungarian punchcutter
Miklós Tótfalusi Kis
(1650–1702),
it retains a strongly
Dutch Baroque character.
The Monotype version
was named for the
Ehrhardt foundry in Leipzig
where the original types
were held in the
early 18th century.

*

The display type,
WEISS ANTIQUA,
was designed by
Emil Rudolf Weiss
(1875–1942)
for the German
type foundry Bauer
and first issued in 1926.
The digital version
used in this book
is from
Adobe Systems.